MW01224596

Peeling the Apple

By

Kylie Gregor-Whitmire

1663 LIBERTY DRIVE, SUITE 200
BLOOMINGTON, INDIANA 47403
(800) 839-8640
WWW.AUTHORHOUSE.COM

First published by AuthorHouse 07/07/05

ISBN: 1-4208-0109-0 (sc)
ISBN: 1-4208-0108-2 (dj)

Library of Congress Control Number: 2004097203

Printed in the United States of America
Bloomington, Indiana

This book is printed on acid-free paper.

I offer up these pages in humble gratitude
to those who have enriched my life
with their love, support, faith, and friendship:

Betsy, my *real* sister.

Erika, Ferl, Hannah, and Noel; the friends of my youth,
my quarter life, middle life, and old age…
years past, present, and many years to come.

Megin, Mindy, and Tricia; more than my colleagues, my friends, my partners
in crime, my saviors from myself.

Grandma Jo, my namesake and divine matriarch of our family.

Of course, Doug.

And especially, Mom.

I love you all eternally.

For Kristene –
who has always held my hand,
through this and so many of life's journeys,
having more faith in me than I have ever
had in myself.

And Jen –
for helping me realize
which parts should stay and
which parts should go; in life and in art.

I am forever grateful.

To my kids:

Without all of you, none of this would be possible.
You have taught me more than you know and have
changed me more than I can ever say.
Your value in my life is immeasurable,
the mark you have left on my heart is permanent,
and my love for you all is undying.

"You have to laugh at yourself,
because you'd cry your eyes out if you didn't."
~Emily Saliers

FOREWORD

This is the book all teachers promise themselves they will write. As each of us enters a classroom and begins to see what it is really like, as we each begin to collect stories in our minds of things that we cannot believe kids would actually say, actually do, we all make a vow to write them all down one day. We make a silent promise to ourselves that we will immortalize our stories, for their humor, their brutality, their unbelievable nature. The difference between me and the hundreds of thousands of other teachers who write books like these in their heads, is that I found the time to write mine down on paper.

This book began as a tribute to my students. When I was faced with leaving the school I had come to know as home and the kids I had come to love for their quirks, their spirits and their downfalls alike, I struggled to find a way to seal them in my history forever. I struggled to find a way to immortalize them, to make them know that I was listening. I also wanted to find a way to show my kids that they are important people, that being in high school does not mean you are stuck in some limbo that fills time before you are an adult and you really matter. I wanted my kids to know that they really matter at any time in their lives. I wanted to pay them the gratitude they deserved for making me the kind of teacher I ended up being when it seemed that not even my professors or my mentors could succeed in that regard.

So, somewhere on the Indiana turnpike on a trip from Ohio to Chicago, this book began. It started quietly in my head, planting a seed that grew into something out of control, an idea that I could not ignore, no longer something I wanted to do, something I had to do. The stories of my brief teaching career began to dance across my mind, selecting themselves as the stories that would occupy these pages. Each student essentially wrote her or his own chapter.

I became a sort of middleman, correction, middlewoman, in this process; scribing the stories as I remembered them, allowing my kids to do the work of being themselves, in my memory as they had in my classroom. The entire process was nearly effortless, because the stories, and the people behind them, were extraordinary to me.

I began to let my students in on the plan to write their stories down. I told them what I was in the process of doing, and their faces lit up. They were amazed that someone could find something in them worthy of writing down. I saw quickly their need to be appreciated in some way, and the excitement that came when they thought of themselves in print. They made it clear that I had made the right decision driving along the Indiana turnpike one Friday after school. My students made it all crystal clear, it didn't matter how, but I was supposed to write this book.

I decided to publish the book through a subsidiary publisher because I wanted to make sure that the project remained true to my vision from the very beginning. I could not imagine trying to sell my kids to an agent or publishing house, getting a letter in the mail saying, "This project just doesn't meet our needs at this time." I did not write this book to fit the needs of a New York publisher or an agent on a power lunch, I wrote it for me, and for my kids. But I had others in mind as well.

When I was in college, I learned quickly that there was no book assigned for any of my classes that gave me what I really wanted, real stories of education. I wanted to know what I would face when I took my place on the other side of the desk. I wanted to know the wildest moments, the most triumphant; I craved the knowledge of a teacher who had been there and could share those stories with me as a novice. I didn't find the book that I was looking for, so I wrote it. As I wrote Peeling the Apple, I thought about what it would have been like to have it when I was in college and I imagined it as a tool for teachers coming into this profession, a rare glimpse into the classroom for people who would eventually be thrown into their own classrooms: excited, but often afraid and unsure.

I also decided that parents should have the opportunity to know what happens in classrooms across America. While I know I am a non-traditional teacher, the thread of caring that goes into teaching is one that is universal. Parents should know that their children are being cared for, delicately and affectionately, academically, and personally. I wanted parents to know that we, as teachers, know when something is wrong, when our students are upset or in trouble, and we want to help in any way we can. We care about their education, but the best of us, care about them as people too.

Finally, I wanted to remind my colleagues, not just the ones in my school, but my colleagues in classrooms from Phoenix to Boston, Seattle to Miami, and all across the United States, why we went into this profession. I wanted a chance to remind all teachers that we are in our classrooms for children, for their enrichment and their advancement, not the money, not the vacations, but the children. Perhaps I wanted a chance to ever so gently say that if we aren't there for the kids, we should get out.

So, while this project began for one very specific purpose, it took shape as something far grander in scope. I opened my own life up for the good of those I have already mentioned: teachers, parents, and students alike. I have put my passions, my feelings for my kids and my life's work, into words, for a greater good, a greater need. Peeling the Apple is a tribute on many levels, the most profound being its function as a tribute to my kids, who will always be my kids, no matter where I am.

Who Am I?

I am a bitch. I am, when I need to be, and I am not afraid or ashamed to admit it. I have always heard the word "bitch" used to describe strong women who know what they want and are not afraid to go after it. Does that make me a bitch? Maybe. When you call me bitch, I am not offended. I like it.

I am a feminist. I live and breathe feminism and am not sure when that became so offensive . A major tenant of feminism is that women are people. I don't think that is such an insane notion.

Am I a ma'am? The first time someone called me ma'am I almost fell over. Does being 25 make you a ma'am? When I look in the mirror I do not see a ma'am. When I look in the mirror I see the same reflection I saw when I was ten, when I was sixteen, when I was twenty. When does that childhood reflection turn into a ma'am? Or does it? Does it make you feel old even when someone who is obviously older than you calls you ma'am?

I am big-boned; robust; healthy; of good stock; well proportioned; I have a pretty face; I am well kept; I have a good personality; I am funny. I have been told all of this at one point or another in my life, meant as ways to make me feel good about at least some part of myself. However, these are all ways of calling me fat. They sound nicer, but they still mean the same thing. When I look at myself I know what I am. I know that when I am wearing a bathing suit I want to curl up and die, or that when I walk things move that should stay still. I don't need someone to try to make me feel better about it, it only ends up making me feel worse. Do I walk around telling people they are ugly? No, I don't, because that is rude, and I was taught not to be rude. Nobody says, "you aren't ugly, but you are proportionately good and bad looking."

I am a woman, 100% through and through. Being a woman affects how I move, think, speak, and live. But don't yell it at me like it is an insult, because it isn't. I love being a woman; I wouldn't have it any other way.

I am a wife, but just because I happen to be one, it does not mean that I will answer when simply called, "wife" like it is my name. Wife is a choice, not something I am because I can be nothing else. It is not my name, but a piece of me.

I am a daughter. My mom calls me daughter sometimes. My dad doesn't call me at all. I am also a child of divorced parents. When I was 2 my "father" decided he didn't want to be that any more. For a while in my early twenties he decided he might give it a try again but as it turns out he didn't like it any better the second time around. I am proof that growing up with one parent does not make you a defective.

I am a sister. Since my parents were divorced so early in my life, no biological link has ever led to this term of endearment. But I have had the opportunity in life to meet a woman who is my sister in all the other senses of the word. Betsy is my sister in my heart. We are like little kids together, because fate screwed up and never let us have a shared childhood. We are making up for lost time.

I am a granddaughter; the kind who doesn't visit her grandmother enough, but loves her as much as any grandchild could. I wear her name between my first and last.

I am a friend. Because I was not blessed with a huge family, I have made my friends my family. My friends are sown together making up the tapestry of my life. They hold my secrets, my memories, my fears, and my dreams. They are the pieces of my life that link me to my past and provide me with hope for the future. I cherish each of them tremendously.

I am a liberal. Dare I call myself a bleeding heart liberal? Perhaps. Each moment of my day I am aware of my liberal existence the way I am aware of my own appendages. It is a part of me.

Am I crazy? You know, I think we all have a little crazy in us. Some people get found out, and some don't. I lock doors five or six times before I am truly convinced they are locked. I make sure no one is going to break into my house and kill me in my sleep. I have arguments with my own demons about who I am and who I want to be. That's what I do. Does that make me crazy? Once, a woman who was a true force in my life called me "crazy person" as a term of endearment. Even though it doesn't sound that endearing, it was. She used it as a preface to tell me to calm down, be the real me, and just breathe. She ran though, when she had to really deal with what crazy looks like. I guess I am what crazy looks like.

I am a writer. From the time I was a young child writing has escaped from me naturally and freely; soft ripples and sometimes rough waves in the sea of my being. The writer in me allows the rest of me to exist, it lets me out of my self-imposed cage. I am the most alive when I am writing. Someone close to me once introduced me to the writer I am, she unlocked the door. Even after she was gone, the writer remained.

I am a teacher. There it is. This is the title I never thought would define me, but now has come to do just that. Teacher is an amalgamation of everything I am. I am a bitch, a liberal, and a feminist teacher. You can shake me up, stir in what you want, add a dash of this and a pinch of that and no matter how long you bake it, I always come out a teacher. You can add any of my attributes to teacher and they fit. However, I have never put crazy teacher on my syllabus. I just don't think there is enough tolerance in the world to wear that one around on a sign. My students figure it out soon enough anyway.

I am a teacher. Though I never imagined I would be, I am. I am proud to be a teacher. I don't believe in that saying, "Those who can, do; those who can't, teach." Who said that any way? I would like to kick that person's ass. I wonder if that genius ever stepped into a classroom with 30 screaming teenagers. Those who can, teach. Anyone who thinks teaching is easy should try it some time. Try finding a way to make teenagers of different levels and learning styles appreciate Shakespeare, or write proficiently, or possess the ability to engage in academic or creative expression. Better yet, try to instill some humanity in teenagers who are growing up in what can be a merciless and inhumane world. I dare you. Anyone who thinks those who can't, teach, walk into my room and stare into the faces of young people whose eyes often beg the question, "What the hell are you here for?" Until you have spent at least a month in my classroom, don't assume that those who can't, teach. Because I can; and I do. I am teacher.

If you believe the afore mentioned sentiment. I suggest you put this book down now. Go get your money back; it won't offend me. This isn't for you. Go find the self-help section; it could do you some good.

Do I sound too harsh? Am I too loud, too obnoxious, too over the top for you? Well, this is who I am. I can be harsh. I can be in your face. Sometimes,

I have to be. That is one of the first things I learned as a teacher. I didn't have a clear sense of myself until I had to stand in front of a group of teenagers constantly judging me, watching my every move. I discovered that I am a person I never thought I could be. I say what I think. I make few apologies. I do not wear my hair in a bun. The traditional stigma of "teacher" is lost on me, and so many teachers of my generation. I am different. We are different. I have been traditionally educated and carry all the proper credentials, but I am not your parents' English teacher. I am not the "norm". When I stand in front of my class I do not hold anything back. I walk into class every day wearing my personality, and my heart, on my sleeve. I am not afraid to let my students see me as a person.

This is my story. It is the story of a woman who found herself in teaching, who learned from her students, who broke the rules and created new ones. This is the story of non-traditional experiences in the most traditional field in the world. This is what teaching looks like, under the peel.

*

"The only people for me are the mad ones, the ones who are mad to live, mad to talk, mad to be saved, desirous of everything at the same time, the ones who never yawn or say a commonplace thing, but burn, burn, burn, like fabulous yellow roman candles exploding like spiders across the stars."

~Jack Kerouac

The Long and Winding Road

When I entered the field of education I had no delusions of grandeur. I came into my profession almost by accident really. I spent my virgin college semester somewhere in Southern Ohio at a school that literally made me feel like a bull in a china shop all the time. It didn't help that I outweighed the typical Jane Q. Co-ed by at least 50 pounds. I walked through the line in the cafeteria and bought raw chocolate chip cookie dough by the pound, blushing a little each time a beautiful long-legged blonde walked by with a salad and a bottle of water. I knew she must have been off to eat her salad somewhere under a tree, daintily dabbing the sides of her mouth with a napkin before briskly walking to the recreation complex for a power workout. I, on the other hand, would most likely emerge from the cafeteria under the weight of a bag filled with books I had no interest in and a plastic container filled with cookie dough that would land directly on my thighs. I would then walk, as I did each day, back to my dorm inhaling the toxins from a freshly lit cigarette. I think I was an aversion to everything that particular school stood for. I smoked cigarettes not because I looked sexy with one hanging from my perfectly lined lips, but because I was addicted to them and had been since I was 16 – a fact I was reminded of each time I was forced to climb the three flights of stairs to my dorm room. I should have known that I was out of place when I saw that my residence hall had no elevator. The worst of it though was not receiving disappointed looks from frat boys as I doled out raw cookie dough, or the smirks from the girls who could tell I actually enjoyed my cigarettes. The worst part of it all was that I had no direction. I had no idea what I wanted to do with my life. So I did the only thing I could do, I declared myself a business major.

I didn't know anything about business as an 18-year-old and I did not think I would be good at it. I had never thought about business as more than an enigma that was out there somewhere in a vast world I would not visit because I didn't have enough money. Maybe that is why I said business when asked, "What do you want to do with your life?" Maybe I thought business equaled money and in lieu of being passionate about much, maybe I thought money would suffice. Or, maybe I answered with business because I thought the suits would cover up the damage the cookie dough would eventually do to my thighs. Whatever the reason, business was the path I cut, without even looking down any of the other paths laid out before me. Business was the answer to a question I didn't want to answer truthfully because I didn't want to put my cigarette out long enough to be left alone in the intimacy of my own thoughts. I had come out of high school burnt out and apathetic like so many other youths do. I was tired of learning and the people who forced me to learn. I was tired of trying to stretch my proverbial wings and soar to some unknown cliché in the sky. I wanted to smoke, to eat, and I wanted a simple way out. I didn't want to think about my future. I was afraid I would never be good at anything and afraid that here, at Perfectly Put Together University, I would be discovered as the kind of kid who never had to work very hard at anything. I would be sniffed out as a girl who had never had to face real struggle. Though I think by being there in the first place, I was wearing a sign that testified to that very fact. I didn't know who I was and I was afraid to find out. What if I was nothing more than a spoiled brat? But I had to be something more, or I would have fit in better with all the spoiled brats that surrounded me at college, staring haughtily down their noses at me.

Needless to say, I did not last long at Perfectly Put Together University. My lips were not full enough, my hair was not straight enough, my butt was too big, my laugh was too loud, and I liked smoking more and more everyday. I knew I should leave before some perfectly boring middle-aged woman named Bambi, clad all in khaki, came politely to my dorm to ask me to leave. I could see the scene playing itself out in my head. I would be sitting in my dorm room, the only safe-haven where I could put on sweatpants and not feel as though someone might stone me in a fit of rage and disgust. The room would be filled with my smoke after tiring of the glares that came from all the healthy kids on campus. Then I would hear a knock at the door. I would answer and see her, a woman in khaki pants and a white shirt, with a camel colored sweater draped over her shoulders. The strand of pearls around her neck would be as white as her teeth because proper ladies, the kind you see in a place like that, would never think of smoking. She would be smiling while politely choking back a cough from the fog of nicotine that swirled about her head. She would see me and I would certainly offend her, the curls on my head trying desperately to escape their place behind my ears. My sweatpants and ripped sweatshirt would make her queasy, but she wouldn't let go of her perfect smile. Then she would politely tell me something unoriginal like, "We have really loved having you here but we think *you* would be happier somewhere else, dear." Which would really mean, the whole school would breathe a sigh of relief to dispose of an unwanted eye sore like me. I wanted to save myself, and Bambi, from such a terribly embarrassing scene.

Thus, in late December, I found myself on the highway that lead out of Perfectly Put Together University and on my way to We Take You As You Are University. A relatively short drive from that hilly campus would lead me to flat faced, familiar Northwest Ohio, and what I hoped would be some sanity and clarity. As I flicked a cigarette onto the campus of PPTU for the last time, I was certain that with each mile my little Honda Civic put between Bambi and me, I would feel a little better about myself. I figured a life without glares, self-loathing, stairs, and cookie dough would do me some good. I was faced with a dilemma though, driving away from that place. What in the world was I going to do with my life? Leaving the harsh environment I had mistakenly applied to would do wonders for my self-worth and self-esteem, but would it answer the question burning beneath all of that? The question made its way through my self-conscious and erupted as my own voice screaming through my brain. The music coming from the tape deck seemed to sing out the question. The sound of my tires on the road hummed it up through my feet and legs, into my torso and left it there pressing down on my chest as I drove. The thought of once again being asked what I wanted to do for the rest of my life turned my stomach and I thought I would have to pull over to vomit before I was even 30 miles into my escape. I turned the volume of the stereo up louder and the screaming in my head only rose in competition. My own mind was teasing me, taunting me, laughing at me for being so indecisive, so void of any real feelings about what I wanted from life. I smoked until my throat hurt, but still nothing. I rolled the window all the way down to let the fresh air filter into the car. As the breeze whipped across my face, blowing my hair into my eyes, I began to hear the question whispering through the gusts. I was being assaulted from all fronts. Finally I was forced to roll up the window, turn down the music and drive in silence, except for the humming of my tires against the road. I was full of the need to do something at my new university that mattered to me, something that I would enjoy. But I didn't know what I would enjoy. I was afraid that once I arrived on my new campus I would only be slightly better off than I had been at the old. Perhaps it wasn't feeling like the fat lady in a circus that really upset me at PPTU. Perhaps it was my lack of direction, my lack of passion about anything.

There was no wheel at my new university that I could spin. There is a wheel in one of my favorite bars. When you spin the wheel, it lands on a drink and that is what you order. It's a fun little game. I wanted a wheel like that to decide what I would study because as registration rolled around I still had no idea. I would have spun the wheel and gone into whichever building held the major the wheel landed on. I was clueless as to what I wanted to do. I was drunk on the fact that I was actually in a place that wouldn't treat me like a social wretch or outcast. I thought that at this new, friendly university, I could buy all the raw cookie dough I desired. However, I never found it in any of the dining facilities. The trade off, cookie dough for my sanity, was one with which I could live. But with that sanity came uncertainty. If I wasn't cut out for business, what could I do, and do well? More importantly, what did I want to do? I had never taken the time to sit down with my own mind and ask myself that very important question. What do I want to do? As a nineteen year old, that should have been a fun question. There are so many options, choices, opportunities – the world is laid out at your feet. It should have been the best time of my life. Instead, it scared the hell out of me. I panicked. What do I want to do? What *do* I want to do? *What* do I want to do? What do *I* want to do? I repeated the question over and over. The answer was always the same; I don't know. I wanted someone to tell me. I wanted someone to point me in the right direction. I wanted someone to tell me what I would be good at. I wanted to spin a wheel. But everywhere I turned, the question was still there, begging to be answered. And I was the only one who could answer it. I had to find my own way.

Honestly, I don't remember how I came to declare my major as education. I would like to think the moment was one in which the heavens opened and the answer came to me like destiny being whispered in my ear. I don't remember this happening. I don't remember the "a-ha!" moment. I just remember it being there. All of a sudden there was the thought of being a teacher, growing in my head like magic. The only link I could think of was that my father was a teacher for a while in his younger years. However, I spent most of my life having no contact with him. I could not have inherited an interest in the teaching profession from a man I barely knew. Did summers off sound like a good gig to me? Yes. But I like to think that I am not shallow enough to select a profession based on the vacation it promises. Did the money sound good? Not really. So what was it that drew me into the field? I guess it was something more abstract than I assumed it would be. When I think back on it, I can see now what might have lead me to teaching. Throughout my whole life there was one subject in school that I loved: English. I enjoyed it because I was good at it and it came easily to me. But I had a feeling that even people who weren't great at writing papers and dissecting symbolism could enjoy it. That feeling translated itself into the idea that maybe, just maybe, I could help people discover the joy I found in expression. Teaching words, ideas, and concepts as a way of showing young people how to express themselves was something I thought I could do. Sharing my enthusiasm and excitement for drama, poetry, and prose sounded perfect. Guiding others through the dreams and dramas hidden in literature as well as facilitating a search for words to tell their own stories sounded incredible. So, I would be an English teacher.

Teaching 101

I never thought I wanted to be a teacher. I did not play school when I was a little girl; I played accountant, lawyer, and cocktail waitress. As different as my childhood dream occupations are from each other, they are even more different from the profession I finally chose as an adult. I never considered myself a teacher, even when I decided that I would teach for a living. I thought that's all teaching was, a job, a way to pay bills, and something I would do every day. I was wrong. Teaching is a way of life, a mindset, a state of being. When I learned this I was in college and the realization worried me. I didn't feel like a teacher. I felt like someone training for a profession, not undergoing a change of heart, mind, and soul. I could see my friends slowly becoming teachers through our training and I wondered why it wasn't happening to me. I listened to the lectures, I took the tests, I did everything I was supposed to do in order to learn how to "be a teacher" and then I realized something, someone can't teach you how to be a teacher. This is not to say that my education classes were not important, because they were. It is necessary to have knowledge in the content area and to know what to do in certain kinds of teaching situations. But there was no class in college that told me what to do when I walked into my own classroom on the first day. There was no class that taught me about the different types of students I would meet. I had to figure all of that out on my own. I had to decide how I would take attendance and how I would deal with students who didn't want to learn. I even bought a how-to book about one's first year as a high school teacher. I looked for answers in the book but they were not there. Every school, every child, every teacher is different. There is no map and no set of instructions. You have only yourself as a teacher, what you learned, and how you decide to impart your knowledge on your students. I learned this quickly. Since I didn't feel like a teacher though, since I didn't feel like it was a part of me, I was worried. I thought the teacher in me would be drawn out through my education, through my classes, but it was not. The teacher in me did not surface until I stood in front of students. In my mind, I looked around the room and it was just them and me. There were the students, staring at me, so by default I had to be the teacher. Then, all of a sudden, the transformation I had been waiting for began.

I did not start to become a teacher until the semester of my student teaching experience. But I was not a teacher on the first day, or during the first week, or even the first month. I walked into my placement with gelatin legs and a sense that I would fall flat on my face. I was terrified. I walked into my student teaching experience like a prisoner walks in front of a firing squad. I had been trained, but I did not feel like a teacher, I did not identify myself as a teacher. I was certain I would fail. For a few weeks I was just a college student observing a "real teacher". I sat in the back of the room and watched my mentor teach his classes and I could tell he was the real deal. I figured that I would certainly become a teacher by watching someone who was so gifted in the profession. Like osmosis, I thought I would soak in his skill. I was certain that by being in the presence of what I considered to be great teaching, I would have to find my own teaching self. I was wrong. When he was teaching, I watched in amazement. He was so natural in front of the class. But while I could recognize that I was in the presence of what I hoped I could become, I didn't identify with it. I didn't think there would be any way I would ever be able to do it myself. I was too nervous, not well read enough, and too afraid that I would have toilet paper hanging from my shoe and the students would all laugh at me. But one day it was time. I had to teach a class. I had to stand up in front of the class and teach them something.

The first time I had to teach a lesson I had to video tape it for my one of my instructors. There would be a record of what happened up there, in the front of the room, a place I had never been. I set the video camera up in the back of the room and I tried to forget it was there. I actually tried to forget the students were there too. I didn't want so many eyes on me, I was too self conscious, thinking that the whole time they would see right through me. I was certain that after I was finished the students would file into the hall and say to one another in hushed tones, "She should have been a business major." But I plowed through the lesson anyway, hoping the camera would not pick up the quivering of my lips or the quaking of my knees. When I got home from school that day I decided I would watch the tape. I cried through the whole thing. I was living with my mom at the time and she heard my sobs and came in my room to see what was wrong. I couldn't even speak. I just sat on the bed with the tears pouring from my eyes. I was awful. I looked like I was faking it and I was afraid that I was. What would I do with my life if I had to fake it every day? I was terrible. I was not a teacher. My mom told me to relax. She assured me that it was the first time and that I would feel better about it the more I taught. I nodded my head, but didn't know if she was right. When the tape was over I continued to cry and contemplated calling in sick the next day. But I had to go back. Something in me said I had to go back. Maybe the second time around I wouldn't pace around the room enough to make my class seasick. Maybe I wouldn't season my speech with "um". Maybe I would fall into a rhythm; one that I could move with and the students could follow. So I went back. I went back to see if it would get better, and it did. Each time I got in front of the class after that first day I felt a little less like I was going to faint and a little more like maybe I could become a teacher, with practice.

But that was student teaching. There was someone there to catch me if I fell. I didn't have to do it all alone. I was armed with a lesson plan book to use as a map and a teacher with 32 years of experience to guide me. Student teaching only made me minimally less scared than I had been about my own classroom responsibility. Even after 15 weeks of observation and practice I felt like I had only a miniscule sense of what I was doing. I lacked the one element with the possibility to make me undergo the transformation from novice to teacher: my own students.

I was hired as a real teacher at the school where I had completed my student teaching. I was nervous but thrilled. I went out and immediately began the speedy process of maxing out my credit card on items for my classroom. The classroom, I thought, was the fundamental building block of learning. Give students a place they want to enter, a place they enjoy being in, and they will learn and love learning. I bought posters and plants and lights to fill my room with happiness and stimulation. If my students loved the room even half as much as I knew the credit card company must, I would be a huge hit. I knew my students would thrive in the environment I would create for them. I worked for days before the first day of school putting my room together. When I was finished, I stepped back and looked at the space I had created. I had achieved what none of my own teachers ever had, the perfect learning environment. My room was bright and colorful. The sun reflecting off the colors on my walls was soothing and the light from a desk lamp was much more friendly than the harsh fluorescent lighting that came standard with my room. I smiled at the space in quiet celebration of what I had done. I had only formalities left. I had to make a syllabus and then I would be ready. I could figure out a syllabus. Rules, regulations, procedures, piece of cake. Then I panicked. I had forgotten one small detail during my blissful interior design escapades. I had to teach my students something. I had never been a teacher before, and no one had come to my room yet to tell me what to teach my students. Suddenly I began to sweat. The room started to go blurry and the colors on my posters blended together, hypnotizing me further into my panicked state. I struggled to keep my knees from buckling under the weight of my own uncertainty. I made a mad dash into the hallway to see if someone was on the way to my room to give me my packet. There had to be a packet, right? Some document that would tell me what to do? Anything? The hallway was empty. What was I going to teach my students? How would I know what to do?

I decided to ask a veteran teacher what I should do. I thought I should find out what the other teachers in my grade level were teaching. I needed a compass, something to guide me as I made my way through the first year. I was calmed when the teacher I spoke to was more than willing to sit down with me and go through her routine, her curriculum. I went into her room feeling hopeful, armed with a pen and paper to record her every word. What I learned from her was disheartening. I thought I was going to get guidance. What I got was a break down of what this particular teacher did in her classroom, but it was so vague, so full of room for interpretation and elaboration that when she was finished I felt as lost as I had when I walked through her door. My meeting with the veteran had done me no real good. I looked everywhere for answers to what I was supposed to teach and the answer I received was always the same, "It is up to you Kylie, as long as you follow the standards." This should have been exciting. I was in a school where I could literally teach my students anything, in any manner I chose. But I wanted someone to tell me what to do. I was desperate for direction. I thought there was a formula. I thought there would be a map, a guideline, something that would take me through what I should do with my students each day. I know now that this was a naïve notion, but fresh out of college, not even yet wet behind the ears, I had no way of knowing what it would be like to be a teacher, especially since I had just spent the better part of my life being the student. So I found myself sitting in a perfectly decorated classroom with the Ohio Department of Education Academic Content Standards for the K-12 English Language Arts Program. I was hopeful that when I opened up what I considered to be the gospel, I would be saved.

I was wrong. I had seen the content standards for Language Arts when I was in college, in fact I had worked with them extensively, making mock lesson plans and units. I thought there might be a different one for "real teachers", but when I opened my classroom copy of the standards, I found that it was just as I had remembered it in college. In the most obscure terms, there it was, laid out before me – what students should learn by the end of each specific grade level throughout language arts. There were a million different ways to fill each standard in the book. So, which one was I supposed to use? I looked in the back of the book to see if there was a section filled with lessons, lists, ideas, something; anything. Nothing. I was on my own. I laid my head down on my desk for what seemed like hours, days, lost in the dilemma of what to do to make my students learn what they needed to learn. I tried to tap into my own high school memories, pulling up what I had learned as a student. I couldn't remember any of it – had I learned anything? I had to find a way to make sure my students didn't forget so easily. But how? What? Then, it started to click. I had been treating education like a mathematical equation and that is not what education is. Until that moment I thought of education in these terms:

1 pretty classroom + 1 newly graduated teacher x list of what to teach = learning.

I had no idea. Learning is not the result of an equation. Learning is the outcome that one hopes to achieve through a process of combining creation, stimulation, motivation, determination, and knowledge. I had to create the ideas that would fulfill the standards for my students. Then I had to find a way to stimulate their minds, a way to make the subject interesting and engaging. I then had to figure out how to motivate students, thus making them understand that what I asked them to do was worthwhile. Finally, I had to use my knowledge to give them the tools, skills, and information they needed to fulfill the learning stage they were at when they walked into my class. And I had to be determined in my plight, because I had to reach all of the students, not just some of them. The equation I started with would have equaled something true educators despise… "playing school". I didn't want to "play school". I wanted to teach. There is a big difference. When you play school you put all of your energy into cutesy handouts and gimmicks, rather than the information, and most importantly, the kids. I had to be a guide, a creator, a facilitator, an educator. My room suddenly didn't matter so much, though I will always believe that students learn the best in an environment in which they feel comfortable. But, I digress.

Newly liberated by the fact that I could use whatever means or ideas I chose to fulfill my duties as an educator, I was slapped in the face by a bit of reality. Schools are a place where resources often determine one's course of action. Teach in a school with plenty of resources, and your job is a bit easier than it would be in a school that is limited by monetary constraints. I happened to find myself in a school with plenty of resources though I still found myself constrained. After I accepted my position, the book orders had already been placed and materials were selected. I found that I did not have as many choices as I thought I would have. Even in the most affluent school districts, textbooks are not entities that change with each passing year, or each new teacher. So I would be using neither a book I selected, nor one with which I was familiar. But of course, schools make sure that you have a copy of the textbook months before you step foot into a classroom. Wrong again. Though it makes little sense, I got the teacher's edition of my textbook two days before I was to walk into a classroom full of students. You work with what you have when you are a rookie. I instantly remembered an amazing teacher I had in college who told us countless stories about her experiences in the classroom. I called up my memories of her classes and tried to find solace somewhere within them. She told us once that sometimes in education, you have to punt. Everything would not always work out the way we wanted it to, or expected it to in the classroom, and sometimes, in a pinch, we would have to punt. I replayed that bit of her wisdom over and over in my head as I wrestled with the fact that I felt under prepared for my first day of teaching, as well as disconnected from the process of selecting my own teaching materials. Her words became my mantra. "Sometimes you have to punt. Sometimes you have to punt. Sometimes you have to punt." Deep breaths. I closed my eyes. I said it out loud so I could hear the words escape my lips. "Sometimes you have to punt."

The mantra, repeated over and over, was calming. When I opened my eyes I felt clearer than I had when I shut them, and found myself ready to attack the task that lay before me. The only obstacle left was that of an orange grammar book. How can an orange grammar book present any kind of roadblock for a teacher? The roots of this evil had been planted long before I even thought of becoming a teacher. The orange grammar book was actually a workbook that each of my students received as a reward for paying their fees. Inside, one could find just about every element of grammar broken down into a few pages with examples and practice. Sounds a bit like a teacher's, especially a new teacher's, dream. For a while I thought the grammar workbook could be my salvation, though I felt in my heart that grammar should be taught through writing. But I was new, and the workbooks had already been purchased, and in public education I assumed it would be a no-no to discard something parents already spent money on. So, workbooks it would be. I delved into them with enthusiasm. I would hate every second but I would plod through, with a smile plastered on my face. I wouldn't be able to let the students see that I detested grammar in isolation, though I knew they would probably share my feelings about it. Grammar was dull, it was mundane, it was interest suicide. I could envision the students shutting down. I would be able to see all signs of life drain from their faces. Right before my eyes, all of the training I had undergone to become a teacher would be plucked from my existence. A well-trained ape could have stood in front of a class and gone through the pages in the grammar workbook. It would be the same, day in and day out. Finally, when I could stand the images of boredom and non-learning no longer, I went to my department chair. I had to plead my case. I had to let him know that there was no way I could teach the orange grammar workbook. Just because it worked for some of the other teachers, it would not work for me. I could not keep a straight face while teaching isolated grammar. Rote memorization of participles and gerunds would do my students no good. And my department chair understood. He agreed in fact. And then he said the magic words, "Kylie, you don't have to use the workbook if you don't want to." There was a chorus of angels in my head. A soft circular light shone around his head. I was set free. The chains fell to the ground. I was a rebel, I had challenged the system and I had won based on my principles of what would be best for my students. I felt like a feminist in the sixties. I was burning my bra… my orange grammar book-shaped bra. And so, the grammar book went, and thus I was able to exert myself as my own creative teaching force. Liberation was truly a beautiful thing.

*

"Teaching without zest is a crime."

~Virginia Woolf

What Makes a Teacher?

In the end, what made me a teacher? Was it the education classes? Was it the Language Arts Course of Study? Was it my liberation from the chains of the orange grammar book? The truth is that becoming a teacher takes a combination of so many things. I used to think my classroom would make me a teacher. I thought I would be able to decorate my way into the shoes of an educator. I also thought I would be able to mold myself into the form of those who came before me. The fact is, there was not one defining moment at which I knew I was a teacher, not when I walked into my classroom for the first time, not when I burned my proverbial bra, not when I gave my first detention. There was no moment, no profound realization that I was a teacher all of a sudden hitting me over the head. But there was something defining about coming into my self as an educator. There was something that made me a teacher, finally, even without horns blowing and balloons flying. There is something you need to become a teacher, something you cannot survive this profession without. It is the simplest and most complex part of teaching. To be a teacher, you need students.

My students have made me a teacher. I thought that classroom rules and seating charts, posters, post-it notes, pens and pencils, a grade book, and lesson plans made me a teacher. But all the props were not enough. Before I met my true identity, my teaching self, I had to have my own classes. It wasn't enough to teach someone else's students. Before I truly became a teacher, I had to meet *my* students. I had to walk into *my* classroom and take control and say something to them. I had to stand in front of my class and be the teacher. I owe my students so much. I owe them a debt of gratitude for teaching me to be the teacher I am, because before them I knew *how* to be a teacher but I wasn't one. I owe my students greatly for showing me that difference. My students have molded my teaching experience and my own teaching self. For that I am truly grateful.

These are my students. Their stories are each as unique as the people behind them. The people in these pages have taught me as much as I have taught them. We have learned together, laughed together, and cried together. These people, *my* students, have brought about amazing change in me. I am the teacher I am, the person I am today because of my students and the experiences they brought me. I realized early that my students were creative, inspiring, intelligent, strong people. Now it is your turn to see them as I did when I met them, as I continue to see them. Welcome to my classroom.

Patrick

Patrick calls me Ogdred Weary. It is the name of a font we found on a website and we thought it was the perfect name for a not-so-proper English woman. When he addresses me as Ogdred Weary, he does so in a splendid English accent. We speak to each other in English accents. It is something we do. Patrick spends his study hall in my room because it is also my planning period. We adopt our English accents often. I don't know why we started it, and it drives other people mad, but to us, it's fun. Once, when another student walked in to drop off a note from the office, he asked if Patrick was an exchange student. After the messenger left, we laughed until we both had tears rolling down our cheeks. I have noticed that Patrick and I are silly together frequently. I think it might have something to do with the fact that my planning period and Patrick's study hall are at the end of the day. We need to let some of the day's events slip away at times. Silliness lets a lot slip away. I think we are silly because we like one another and it is fun to have someone to be silly with, even if that someone is one of your students. When Patrick walks into my classroom ninth period, I smile. I know that there will be no stress, no yelling, and no worries. He told me once that walking into my room put him instantly in a good mood, no matter how his day had been. I like the thought that coming into my classroom can be a pleasurable experience for a teen. I think that means I am doing my job.

Patrick is my friend. He was my student in the beginning, during my first year of teaching, but since then he has become my friend. However, one of the primary lessons I learned while studying to become a teacher was that teachers and students couldn't be friends. I was told, nodding in passive agreement as professors drilled the information into my ripe brain, that in order to be an effective teacher and authority figure, I could not befriend a student. Every teacher educator I ever encountered told me to draw a line in the sand, on the tile floor, or in other words, between teacher desk and student desk. I had a vision of The Berlin Wall, separating me from my students. I thought of caution tape around me to show my students that I, the person, was off limits to them. I needed a bubble; I would be the bubble teacher. I would live in a bubble and not let any student venture inside. My students could not know my first name, they could not hear my stories; I was to be their teacher and nothing more. Teacher and person were two different things. This is one of the lessons I have fully rejected since becoming a teacher. I found in a short time that students don't want to listen to a bubble. Also, if *people* didn't teach students, then computers would and I would be quickly out of a job. I needed to be human in order for the students in my class to trust me, to listen to me, and to respect me enough to do more than exist and breathe. Students have to do more than breathe to learn anything; and a teacher has to do more than act as a roboticized version of an encyclopedia.

So I told the students my stories, they guessed my first name, and I wasn't fake with them. When they asked me something I didn't know, I told them I didn't know and we learned the answer together. I didn't pretend to be an infallible teaching machine. I thought for a while about trying to lie my way to perfection, but I decided that teachers also needed to be as honest as possible with their students. I laughed with my students all the time, and I still do. They need to laugh sometimes. They especially need to laugh at themselves and even at me. I let the students see that I was a person with experiences and feelings. I let them see that I was real. Many of them were shocked at first. Once, as a student was walking down the hall singing a popular rap song, I started singing along. The girl stopped dead in her tracks, staring at me. She smiled and said, "You know that song?" I replied by assuring her that I crawled out from under the rock where all teachers live to join society every once in a while. I think it is important to let the students know that someone in their lives is interested in what they do and think and listen to and watch on television. In order to understand my students I knew I had to put some effort in and let them understand me too. Students respond when you are willing to be open with them. That is how I came to truly know Patrick. He taught me what opening up to students can do.

I said before that Patrick is my friend and that is true. Patrick is a lot more too. Patrick is a musician, an activist, a pagan, and Patrick is gay. I learned about Patrick quite quickly. I let him feel safe enough to open up to me, and one day he did. First, he explained his paganism. One day, sitting on a desk across from mine, Patrick matter-of-factly said, "I am a witch." I will admit that when Patrick first told me he was a pagan, I thought he was a bit weird. I envisioned him at home, with a wart on his nose, wearing a black pointed hat, and stirring a brew in his cauldron with a broom. A high school witch? In my class? I didn't think so. But Patrick explained his pagan beliefs to me, that he was capable of researching and performing spells, but that he was "not that kind of witch". Patrick was the kind of pagan who wanted to find a way to bring out the good in the world. Even if I didn't completely identify with what he was saying, and I didn't, I was interested in it. I saw before me a young man who was different from everyone around him and he was not afraid to show those differences, he celebrated them, because they make him who he is.

Shortly after the start of my first year of teaching, Patrick started to stay after class to chat with me. One day we found ourselves in a conversation that somehow lead to the words "I'm gay" slipping from his lips. I don't remember what the original conversation was about – I have no idea how we got to "I'm gay", but we did. And there it was, Patrick was gay. He had come out to me, there in my classroom after a rowdy discussion of poetry, or the novel as a genre, or Shakespeare... it doesn't matter now. A student had just come out to me and I learned, from the conversation, that I was the only adult to be privy to this information, to know his true self. I was caught off guard on a couple of levels. First of all, I didn't consider myself an adult in the way that students could look at me and see me as a person totally separate in generation from themselves. When I looked in the mirror I still saw the same girl I saw in high school. But I *was* separate from them, and they saw me that way. And secondly, a student just brought me into his confidence in an incredibly personal and intimate way. I was stunned; I was in awe; I was honored. And Patrick just kept talking through the revelation that he was gay. He kept on with his story, he didn't stop to wait for my reaction or to see if I would gasp or look at him through squinted eyes trying to hide feelings of hate or disgust. To me, the fact that Patrick continued to speak through this huge confession meant that he knew I would be okay with what he said, and I was. It was as if he knew before he told me he was gay that I would accept him no matter what. And he was right. The event was rather uneventful really. He said it; I listened; he moved on with the rest of his story, and then scampered off to his next class. That was it. "I'm gay, see you later, have a nice day."

After Patrick left the room I sat at my desk, motionless. Was I the kind of teacher kids could come to and share their secrets? Had I created myself as the one person in some kids' lives that they could talk to about anything? Could my students see that little would rattle me; that I would be accepting of whoever they were, whoever they wanted to be? It appeared as though Patrick saw me that way. So I had to ask myself if I wanted to be that kind of teacher. Was I prepared for kids to tell me things that I might not want to hear? Or, not so much things I didn't want to hear, but things I didn't know if I *should* hear, according to my teacher education? Was I ready to be a little bit more than a teacher when my students needed that? Could I be a confidant, a stand-in parent, an ally? I knew after a few moments of clouded fog in my head, that I didn't have a choice. I was that kind of teacher, by nature. I couldn't stop students from talking to me if they needed someone to listen to them. I couldn't pretend not to be human to kids who needed some humanity. And I couldn't turn the switch from person to teacher continuously on and off. It didn't matter what my teacher educators told me; I was who I was. Patrick obviously told me he was gay for a reason. Maybe he needed to hear the words come from his mouth. Maybe he needed to say something that made him more real to someone. Perhaps he needed to have someone see him, really *see* him. Whatever the reason, whatever the course that lead me to the moment when Patrick told me he was gay, I had become the kind of teacher kids could talk to, about anything. It didn't feel wrong to me. It felt like something I needed to be, something the kids needed me to be. I felt comfortable in the role I had landed in after my discussion with Patrick. I felt like I was being me, the me I had been trained to shut off when I walked into my classroom. And in no longer denying myself as a person, but embracing the person I was and allowing it to flow into the teacher I had become, I felt like I was able to give my students something they needed. I could give them something more than pronouns and participles, symbolism and sentence structure. I could give them something they could use a lot more in their future than they would ever use their ability to underline a gerund. Who underlines gerunds any more anyway? Who ever did, other than antiquated English teachers? I could give my students someone who listened to them and made them feel okay when others made them feel wrong.

I didn't know what kind of teacher I would be when I first started in this field because I didn't know what kind of teacher I should be. I didn't know what kind of teacher I was allowed to be. Patrick is the person who first showed me who I was as a teacher. He showed me what kind of teacher I *could* be. Patrick showed me the combination of two halves of me that I was told to keep separate. He showed me that I was person and teacher all in one, that I couldn't separate those two parts of my being because they both made up who I was. Patrick held up a mirror and when I looked into it I saw an image of me reflected. An image of me that I hadn't seen before stared at me. I was not the same girl who overate cookie dough just a few years before, or hid in her dorm room because she was too afraid of what people would say about her. I was now a woman who could make the lives of young people easier and more bearable. This, I knew, was a great task. I knew it would not be easy, and I knew it could fill my heart and break it at the same time. But I didn't care. As the mirror in Patrick's hand told me, you can't lie about who you are; Patrick didn't, and neither could I.

I was ecstatic when I got home from school the day Patrick told me he was gay. He had given me a unique gift, the gift of his trust and his confidence, as well as the gift of my own identity as an educator. I was one of few people he had trusted with his true self, his being, and his identity. This bonded me to him immediately. I felt like I owed him the promise of always being someone he could come to with anything, and I silently made that promise in my head. In addition, he gave me the ability to see myself as I never had before. I knew that I would maintain a relationship with Patrick even after he left my class. He had become someone special to me, someone who taught me something about the teacher and the person I was. I didn't know I was someone worthy of the kind of trust and confidence Patrick bestowed in me, but in his own way, Patrick showed me a reflection of myself as someone I liked being.

Patrick was a student first and he was gay second. Eventually Patrick became, and is to this day, my friend. The conventional student-teacher relationship does not exist between us. He does not see me as an authoritarian imposing my rules on him and forcing upon him lessons he will not use. I do not see him as someone I have to control and restrict. We see each other as equals. Our relationship is based on the fact that we can both learn something from the other. He has taught me perhaps as much as I have taught him. Patrick and I respect one another. I do not see him as inferior because he is a student, and I do not expect him to see me as superior because I am a teacher. We are people who exist on a similar plane. We laugh everyday. We laugh at ourselves, and at each other, and we laugh at the world around us. I have fun with Patrick. We are human together; defying what my textbooks in college told me was possible. We break the rules everyday with our relationship; rules, perhaps, that in our situation, were meant to be broken.

Patrick is a senior now and he is ready to go out into the world. He will change the world as he has changed me, this much I know. Patrick has left a mark on me that cannot be erased or forgotten. He taught me about myself and taught me that it is okay to be the person you are in any situation. To be an openly gay high school senior in Ohio is not easy, but Patrick has done it with grace and humor. He is resilient in his beliefs and in his ideas of the way the world should be. Patrick is an advocate to stop violence against women, he gives of his time and energy to help causes that are bigger than most people realize. He fights for people who might not ever be willing to fight for him. I admire Patrick a lot more than he knows; for he has touched my life in a way I cannot describe. I wish everyone knew Patrick. I wish everyone could see him when he laughs and when he makes a mockery of a society that will not accept him as the amazing human being he is, simply because he breaks the "rules". Above all, we are all human. That is something Patrick taught me. We are not young, old, Pagan, Christian, man, woman, straight, gay, teacher, student. We are people. And Patrick the person is fabulous, talented, smart, fancy, feeling, colorful, mystical, magical, funny, playful, and real. He is my fabulous, talented, smart, fancy, feeling, colorful, mystical, magical, funny, playful, real student... *and* friend.

*

I remember when Mary was trying to get into Ohio State. She brought me her entrance essays at least 5 times. She wanted so badly to move away from her hometown and start a new life. She wanted to have something for herself that no one else could touch. As I read through her essays I remembered feeling that same way when I was her age. She was able to tap into the feeling of being on the verge of something amazing in her essays. She came shining through in her words as the true, real, amazing young woman she really is. When she got accepted, she left her class to find me in the school Media Center. She was clutching the letter in her hand and couldn't wait for me to read it. I was so proud of her. I knew she would get in but she had been so unsure of herself. The acceptance from Ohio State was the boost she needed to see who I have always seen in her.

I have loved Mary since I first met her. She is the kind of young woman who is easy to love. She puts her heart and soul into so much of what she does. She and I have always had a relationship going far beyond teacher and student. Mary has not had an easy life. She came from a divorced family like I did and we can identify with one another on that and many other levels. We learned early on that we could learn from one another and lean on one another as well. Mary came to me one day with tears in her eyes and asked if she could have a hug. I asked her what was wrong and she replied by saying, "I'm just having a really bad day and I needed a hug so I came to see you." I gave her the hug she asked for, and it made me feel good too. On my worst days Mary can make things better for me too. No one ever told me there would be students like Mary in my teaching experience. She was a pleasant and welcomed surprise.

Audrey

A true paradox occurs when two opposites coexist harmoniously. I had never seen a true-to-life paradox until I met and came to know Audrey. Audrey is the complete embodiment of all that I have ever spoken out against in society. She is the manifestation of what I have always known to be contrary to my beliefs. I am the kind of person who wears a lot on my sleeve. It is difficult for me to hide my political stances on certain issues and somewhat impossible to mask them on others. I have always seen myself as a person who thrives when surrounded by liberal minds liken to my own, and rages when faced with opposition. I am not the kind of person who cannot take others' positions into account with respect, but am the kind of person who at times feels unable to identify with people who do not share my own beliefs and convictions. I have seen this at times as a personality flaw, but at other times as something that is natural. I think the world exists largely in this same mindset. We identify ourselves with people who share the beliefs we hold dear. People come together through shared belief, thought, and opinion. I think this is human nature. Therefore, it is also human nature to be in conflict, at least internally, with those who speak contrary to all that you believe. Before I became a teacher I was rarely challenged in this facet of my being. It is easy to surround yourself with people who are like you in normal society. But, in the society of the American High School, you are surrounded by all different kinds of students. Thus, you are surrounded by people who have vastly different views than your own. Some might think that in a high school classroom it is only the teacher who holds strong opinions about society, religion, and politics. I discovered in my first year of teaching that this notion is completely false. Students are largely, in most cases, a product of their parents' doctrines. Students come into class with a background built by parents, church, guardians, and socioeconomic status, just to name a few. As a teacher, I found early on that students' beliefs and opinions can often escape into the air when it is least expected. As a teacher with strong convictions myself, what was I supposed to do when those convictions contradicted my own? Audrey helped me to answer that question.

Audrey's father is a pastor. In fact, Audrey's father is perhaps one of the most well known individuals in the area around our high school. When I finally realized who Audrey's father was (three years after I met her) I felt like an idiot for not making the connection between their last names earlier. He is the kind of man who everyone thinks they know, who everyone has heard of, but perhaps few really understand. I don't know that it would be fair to call him a celebrity, but in small town USA he may be as close as it gets. I had also heard of her dad's church when I realized Audrey's connection to our celebrity pastor. Various accounts of the church had come forth through the years, that it had a huge congregation dedicated wholeheartedly to their faith, and to their pastor. Some people said it was "cultish" to put it bluntly, because of the devout following, but I always thought that was too harsh of a description. We are all passionate about something, and it seemed that there happened to be a great number of people passionate about Audrey's father, his message, and his church. His church was an institution in the area. It was a place, an enigma, that many did not understand, thus the harsh judgment. I have always known that people fear what they do not understand and while I always hoped I was the kind of person who would reject that stereotype, I fell victim to it in this circumstance. I knew of Audrey's dad's church long before I met Audrey, long before I decided to become a teacher, or had my own classroom. Pastor Freeling's name brought about recognition and reaction in everyone. So, in an effort to be less judgmental and more informed, I decided one day in college to watch one of his sermons on television. I watched the sermon not because I felt like it was meant for me, not because I was overly religious, but because I wanted to know what is was like to be affected by him rather than let others make my opinions for me. I wanted to be able to form my own opinions about him. When I watched the sermon I found that he was a phenomenally powerful speaker. I saw charisma in him that was unmatched by anyone else I knew of. I was enamored. Though I didn't necessarily believe in all that he believed in, I respected him for speaking so eloquently and so passionately to people who did. He was radiating on the television screen. I was excited while I watched, because of my own passion for words, all words, and he spoke them so beautifully. I understood why people would flock to him, why so many people would line up to listen to him deliver his sermons. I might have been one of them in another life, but even while I was not a member of his congregation, I understood now why so many were. I decided that no one had a right to judge him or his congregation without real knowledge to support an attack.

Years after seeing that televised sermon, Pastor Freeling's daughter walked into my Honors English class. I did not know Audrey Freeling. I did not connect her last name to her infamous father until two years later. When she walked into my class she was simply one of my students, in one of my first classes as a teacher. On my first day of teaching, in third period Honors English class, I saw something unique. When I looked out over the sea of new faces staring at me, Audrey's stood out. Her eyes were gleaming, the smile on her face was genuine and there was a glow about her. She looked interested. She was not filled with apathy like the rest. She was not caught up in the smell of freshly sharpened pencils or the squeak of new school shoes. She looked at me with intrigue. She stared hard with conviction that I had something valuable to impart on her, and she was waiting patiently to find out what that was. Audrey was eager and ready to start some journey with me as the guide. She did not seem afraid, even though I was afraid. I was terrified that I would have no idea where to take my students. Audrey's was the kind of face that would catch any teachers' attention, the kind of face that should make all of us stop and be thankful that there is at least one student out there who wants to know what we have to say. I felt more confident when I saw Audrey than I did before she walked in because she seemed confident in me, when my own confidence in myself was wavering. I did not want to let her down. I didn't want Audrey to know that my mouth was dry and that I could feel the sweat building up underneath my arms. I was terrified but I felt an obligation to make her think I knew what I was doing. So, I faked it.

The truth is, on my first day of teaching, I had no idea what I was doing. I did not know what to say to the people staring back at me. I did not know who they were or where they came from, all I knew was that their very existence terrified me. They sat there as proof that I didn't study hard enough when I was in college. They were constant reminders that I could have done more with my collegiate experience. Now, I owed these young people an education and I did not know how to deliver my debt. I did not know how to even speak to them. I was frozen. I had been up since 4 o'clock in the morning and I had been pacing the halls of the school since 6 a.m. No amount of nicotine or caffeine made a difference when the students walked in that first day. I thought I had it all figured out. I thought that if I decorated my room and made a nice looking place for the students to sit that I would be able to wing the rest. I fell victim to what I call "teacher myths", similar to the idea that I could "play school" and it would work. I thought that I had it figured out when I made my seating charts and passed out note cards on which the students could record their contact information. Beyond that, I thought some stroke of genius would hit when I saw the faces of people begging knowledge. I thought I could wing it. There was no winging it – and when I stood in front of my own students for the first time was when I knew that to be a certainty. I had to figure out how to take my passion for literature, for the written and spoken word, for the world that all of my curriculum could open up for my students and translate it into something they could grasp. I had to make my passion tangible, I had to make it something that my students could take hold of, wrestle with, something my students could put in their pockets and take with them when they left my room. I knew I had to do that. But I didn't know how. What I did know on that first day was that while I might be able to fool her for one day, I could not fool Audrey for long. I saw a sparkle in her eye, something that let me know she was sharp. I knew she got it. That allusive "it" that we all hope to get someday, but wonder if we ever will. I also knew I would have to get it too. Or I would be in serious trouble.

As the class periods passed into days and days into weeks, I came to truly know and experience Audrey. She was unlike anyone who went to my own high school. She was unlike any student I ever imagined. Throughout her time in my class, Audrey answered every question I asked with certainty. Her conviction exuded from her. Audrey was brimming over with confidence and glowed when given the opportunity to speak her mind or engage in a battle of wits with another classmate. She was what I imagined the perfect student would be. I thought she couldn't be real. I was waiting for something to ruin her. I didn't know if she was going to slash my tires or toilet paper my house, but she was too perfect, she was too good to be true.

Then it happened. I discovered what I had been waiting for. During Audrey's class one day we had a brainstorming session through which the class would select debate topics. I decided to engage my Honors classes in debates early in the school year in order to make them comfortable with their own opinions and their own voices, two things they would need desperately for the remainder of their time in my class. I also felt strongly that teenagers had a right to express their opinions. I felt that it would allow them to begin caring about their world early, so that later, when they were called upon to make decisions by casting a ballot, they would be ready to latch onto something they were passionate about. I also thought it was extremely important for them to feel like they could be heard in some way. Teenagers, like any one else, need to know that they are valued; that their opinions matter. They are too young to vote, too young to drink, and when I get them, too young to even drive.

But teenagers are not too young to have stances on many different issues; and often, their opinions are rooted in very strong feelings, beliefs, and convictions. Everyone has a right to expression, and all too often teens are silenced. When I was a teenager I had a few teachers who let me know it was okay to have a voice and to let it be heard. I remember being at my best in high school when a teacher let me talk. I had so much to say and I wanted to know what my own voice and my own convictions sounded like. I wanted to see the reactions of my peers and my teachers and know that I was more than just a kid in a classroom spitting back information about books. I wanted to give my students the voice I was allowed to share when I was their age, in hopes that it would make them as passionate about the world as it had made me; this was one of my highest goals as an educator. However, I didn't prepare myself for students who would have voices as loud as mine, or students who would say things with which I couldn't agree. Hearing voices that spoke in contrast to my own put me in a quandary. If one of my students spoke out against something I believed in or spoke in favor of something I did not, what could I do? My instincts as a human being, as a liberal thinker, would be to argue, to show why their arguments were flawed. But my instincts as an educator were to celebrate the fact that my students had something to say. The educator in me would go out in the hall and scream, "My students have views and they aren't afraid to share them with the world!" So who would win in this situation? The liberal or the educator? If faced with a student who spoke out against me, which side of me would come through? I didn't know who would show up.

During the fall semester of my rookie year of teaching, I was still wet behind the ears. I hadn't beaten the habit of breaking into a sweat when I looked into the eyes of twenty-five 14 and 15-year-olds. When I drove to school I still thought that it wouldn't be terrible if I was in just a small car accident. I remember driving to school that first semester and thinking that if I could just bump into another car and break my leg, at least I wouldn't have to go to school for the day. It was a sick thought, I know now, but I fell victim to thinking of desperate action since I was living through a situation that still made me a bit uncomfortable. My feet were in the water but that seemed to only make them slippery. I didn't feel I had a strong hold of what I was doing. As I said before, there isn't a rulebook for teaching. Someone doesn't come in and sit you down, hand you a schedule for what to teach each day, ask you for questions, and leave. You walk into a classroom, get your class lists and you sink or swim. I felt like I was sinking. In fact, I was fairly certain of it. At night I had dreams of a classroom full of students staring at me, burning holes into me with their eyes. In the dream, I would open my mouth to speak to them and nothing would come out. They would begin to laugh and point at me. Suddenly as they laughed I melted into a puddle on the floor. Then, as the students continued to laugh, the custodian would come in and throw the sawdust they put on vomit when kids get sick in school onto the puddle I had become. I would be soaked up by the sawdust and swept away just in time for a teacher who knew what she was doing to be ushered into my classroom and take over. It was a grim dream but I was certain it would be my fate. I woke up in a cold sweat at least three nights a week during my first semester of teaching.

I don't remember if I had that recurring dream the night before I brainstormed debate topics with Audrey's class. But when class began that day, I could feel my arms, legs, and fingertips, the steady rhythm of my own breathing, and my heart pounding in my chest. I had not turned into a puddle. So I had to do something with the students who stared back at me, certainly waiting for me to fail so I could become humorous lunchroom discussion. Debate topics, yes. Ask kids what they want to talk about and they will certainly tell you. This would work. I loved to debate when I was their age, and even as an adult I still felt that sparring about controversial issues was a great thrill. I decided I wouldn't tell my students that debating in class would actually cover almost all of the state curriculum standards for their age level. That would have sucked the fun out of the activity like a vacuum. They would have hated it if they thought they had to do it to make the State Department of Education happy. So I let it seem fun, and it worked. Almost immediately the students dug into the activity. We began a list on the chalkboard of all of the topics they thought would be good debate material. Abortion, legalization of marijuana, euthanasia, gay marriage and adoption, cloning, and prayer in schools were among the topics that found their way to the voting table. I was amazed at what the students came up with and amazed at how passionate they seemed about each topic they suggested. What was extremely interesting about the whole class period was the fact that as each topic was introduced; the students began to debate the topic right then and there. When one person suggested a topic, for example same-sex marriage, the other students vocalized their opinions immediately. Knowing that controlling teen urges can be next to impossible, I let them go. What culminated was a series of full-on mini debates, on whatever topic was broached. I welcomed this experience because it eased the students into what they would do later. It prepared them to feel comfortable challenging the beliefs of their peers, their teachers, parents, or even themselves. What I found out on this particular day in Audrey's class was that I had been right about her from that very first day. She had a spark, a fire that was ignited by the opportunity to express herself on controversial issues. The day Audrey's class brainstormed debate topics was my first big challenge as an educator and as a liberal. It was the first time my duality of self was called forth. Audrey made me step to a new level and learn a crucial lesson about myself.

One of Audrey's classmates brought up the topic of abortion not long after the bell rang to begin class. The room was abuzz with the fledglings of discussion and ideas when a strong voice came from somewhere in the middle. The voice was sharp with calm resilience. It was not angry or militant, but confident and stern. It was the voice of someone who viewed their words as truth, no questions asked. I looked out into the sea of desks in my room for the origin of the voice. I could see other students mimicking my search. We all looked together for the source of the words that had now silenced the rest of the class. Our eyes seemed to land on Audrey all at once. She sat straight up in her chair and looked around as she spoke, addressing anyone and everyone at the same time. Audrey's position was crystal clear. Abortion under any circumstance was wrong. She was adamant, stating mostly religious reasons for her beliefs. The conviction in her voice made her words seem like undisputed fact. To Audrey her words were fact. Her religion told her that abortion was a sin, and she agreed without qualms or questions. She was as strongly opposed to abortion as I was in support of a woman's right to do as she wished with her body. As Audrey spoke I was faced, for the first time in my teaching career, with a firm challenge of my beliefs, convictions, and opinions. I was stunned. A freshman in high school was unintentionally challenging the very fiber of my being. And she was doing a remarkable job. As she spoke, I wondered which part of me was going to come forth, the liberal or the educator. My mind was in overdrive. My own convictions were screaming in my head, citing Roe Vs. Wade and lamenting at the thought of taking what I considered to be a step back in history. Who would win, the liberal or the educator? Would the liberal allow Audrey to speak without challenge? Would the educator allow her to be silenced with my own opinions? In a flash the liberal and the educator melted into one person. The liberal in me played devil's advocate, not to tear down Audrey's beliefs, but to push her further in her expression. The educator in me applauded her when she made a point that none of her peers could contradict. Audrey's quickness of expression put many to rest that day, and when no one could spar any longer, I let the discussion die, knowing that it was the students' time to be heard, not mine. The liberal educator in me thought that was an excellent course of action. Audrey spoke passionately on each of the issues she entertained in class. She was eloquent and passionate with every word. I had never heard anything like Audrey expressing herself in my classroom. I couldn't help but be enamored by the way she expressed herself. She was showcasing the exact opposite of everything I spent my life believing in. She was an affront to all of my convictions. In her words, Audrey represented what

I thought was wrong with the world. But she did it with such grace I actually found myself respecting her *and* her beliefs.

Everyone has flaws and there are few of my own that I am afraid to face upfront and take ownership of. I am not afraid of my flaws, always hoping that I will be able to improve on them. One such flaw is that I have, at times, found it nearly impossible to entertain beliefs contrary to my own. I know this trait to be one that can turn people off like the flick of a switch. However, I have spent enough time considering myself the fundamental democratic feminist to find conservative values hopeless and foolish. In fact, I have often found myself violently opposed to conservative ideals and specifically those who embody them. Audrey embodied every conservative ideal I had ever felt strongly against. But something happened to me when Audrey was speaking. I listened to her and while my instinct was to judge her, to leap into defense of my liberal existence, I instead respected her for speaking her mind. I will admit now that it was not a natural exercise for me in the situation. I had a hard time respecting ideas that did not reflect my own, and while I always knew it was very politically incorrect, I was at times guilty of shutting down to contrary beliefs. I never would have imagined myself, before hearing Audrey speak, listening to someone passionately express beliefs that made my skin crawl at best. But listening to Audrey, I was amazed. She was so young, yet so strong in mind and conviction. I noticed something else as well; she did not speak down to those who disagreed with her, sometimes openly and violently. Audrey listened to everyone. I was speechless. I watched the interchanges silently from my table in the front of the room. Other teachers may have silenced the class, careful not to let them stray too far from the task at hand, but it was far too intriguing for me to halt the conversations of my class. Other students attacked Audrey, asking her how she could believe what she did. They were relentless. Those on Audrey's side of the fence shot back with just as much venom as had been spat at them. But Audrey was calm. She looked her opposition in the eye, not with intimidation, not with disgust or disapproval, but with respect, and she listened to them. She displayed something I knew was possible but had often been unable to display myself. Audrey was the picture of grace. She separated opinions from the people who expressed them. She did not see individuals as hostages of their beliefs. Audrey showed that despite her strong convictions to the contrary of what they said, those who felt differently than she felt had every right to express themselves. I saw something in her that day that I admired. I saw a duality in Audrey. I saw a young woman, full of ideals, respecting wholeheartedly the ideals of others. I had not, in more than twenty years of life, been able to show such poise and repose in the same sort of situation. And through Audrey's duality, I discovered my own.

What Audrey taught me without even realizing it was invaluable. She taught me that the harmonious existence of two opposing viewpoints is possible. I never thought that to be so. I thought I had to always surround myself with those who saw life and the world from my perspective. I was such a fool. I learned from Audrey that surrounding yourself with various opinions, including ones with which you disagree, is not only intellectually stimulating, but self-affirming. It is through the exposure to many beliefs that your own can be solidified or challenged or changed. If no one ever challenges your beliefs, how do you know how strongly you hold them true? I learned from Audrey that I am able to be more open minded than I ever thought I could be. I learned that I was an elitist before I met her and I didn't recognize that part of me. Audrey taught me that the human being I considered myself to be, the human being I preached that I was, had some growing to do and she helped to fertilize that growth.

To this day Audrey is one of the students I have remained closely connected to. I have spent two years seeing her daily and we share a respectful and open relationship. One of my greatest compliments came from Audrey after knowing her for only one year. She told me that after being in my class she wanted to be an English teacher again, after being turned off by a teacher in her past. Audrey, it seems, found something in me liken to what I found in her, inspiration. She is by far one of the most remarkable people I know. She is refreshing and wise, kind and strong. I am in awe of the woman she is and the woman she is growing to be. She is a woman I respect and call equal. We joke from time to time about how opposite we are, and how well we continue to get along. Others can't believe how fluidly we can exist in each other's company. To us, the notion that we could ever dislike one another based on conviction alone is funny. We both represent so many things that the other finds fault with. But we do not find fault with one another. We find sameness in each other. And we really are the same in many ways. We are both passionate people, and while we are passionate about some contradicting issues, we share a passion for writing and poetry and life. Audrey keeps me on my toes, just like she did the first day she walked into my room. She challenges me to be more than I think I am. She is the kind of student and the kind of person the world needs more of. I am fortunate to know her, and to disagree with her. I am a better me because of Audrey.

*

Amy's dad died when she was only two years old. After her own father's death, she came to know and love the man to whom her mother was remarried. During Amy's junior year of High School, her stepfather died. I saw her in the hall just after his death as she was coming to get homework from the absences surrounding her stepfather's funeral. When I hugged her she cried even harder than she had been when I first saw her. Her strength emanated though, as she told me she was more worried about her brother than herself, and wanted to make sure he was okay. She cried for the death of her stepfather and the loss and pain her brother was feeling much more than she cried for her own grief. That is the way Amy is. She takes care of other people even when she should let someone take care of her. For her strength and her big heart, Amy is an incredibly special young woman.

Max

When I told Max that I was writing a book about teaching I also told him that a chapter of the book would focus on him. He asked me what his chapter would be about and I told him it would be about the experience of knowing him. He looked me dead in the eyes and asked if I was writing about the students I really cared about. In his own way he was asking me if I cared about him. I told him that yes, though I care about all of my students, the ones I was including in the book were particularly special to me. Perhaps of all the students I have met on my short journey through education, Max is the one who tugs at my heart the most. There are days when I just want to reach out and give him a hug. When Max isn't in school, I miss him. I look forward to seeing him each day because he makes me smile. I have been affected by a lot in my career, but Max has laid his handprint on my heart. Max has made me realize that I can care for one of my students more than I care for myself. He has made me see that in the seemingly cold heart of a feminist lies an instinct to love someone who needs to be loved. Max has shown me that caring about someone enriches your own life as much as it enriches the lives of those around you.

Since I began teaching, I have had the unique opportunity to teach a class in conjunction with one of the Special Education teachers in my school. Tara Wyland is responsible for all of the freshmen students on Individualized Education Plans in my school. In other words, Tara is responsible for the students who have learning disabilities and behavior or emotional disorders. Each year she selects a freshman teacher with whom she feels comfortable placing her students. I have had Tara's kids in class for two years. Some of the people in our building would see this as a punishment. They would never admit to that statement, but I know it to be true. With Tara's kids comes a little more paperwork and the need for a lot more patience. However, I have never seen the placement of Tara's students in my class as a burden or an inconvenience. I have enjoyed the opportunity to help kids that other teachers have written off. I like teaching kids who some say cannot learn, because they can learn, in the right environment. I take the fact that Tara has trusted me with her students as a challenge and as a great compliment. In placing her faith in my teaching ability, she affirms what I do each and every day. I have found that education is often a thankless career and in her way Tara thanks me each day by allowing me to teach her students. This is how I came to know and to love Max.

Max walked through my door during my third year of teaching. I didn't know what to think of him when he first sat down in my classroom. He was louder than the other students and it was apparent that he craved their attention. Max said the kind of things that some people think but do not vocalize, seemingly because he just wanted to be heard. During the first week of school I discovered that Max had a unique "talent". He ate change. I know that sounds odd. I didn't believe it when I first found out either. I couldn't conceive of someone swallowing coins: quarters, dimes, nickels; he was not discriminatory. Some of his classmates told me that once, on a class trip, he ate so much change that he set off the metal detectors in the airport. I was appalled. I jumped to conclusions and thought Max was strange and I felt myself pull away from him. I didn't understand the type of child that would put dirty, filthy coins into his mouth and swallow them. I asked him to stop, mostly because I wanted to make sure he did not disrupt my class showcasing his disgusting habit. He was like a mini freak show. Boys in class would dare Max to eat a certain number of quarters and he would not hesitate. I caught him one day, about to swallow a small handful of coins. I remember yelling out to him, startling him to paralysis. He sat there, looking up at me, smiling quizzically as though he could not understand why I would ask him not to eat the dare. I explained that while he was in my classroom he was not to put money in his mouth. He lowered his hand and emptied it onto the desk. The other students groaned as they had missed their chance to see such a feat.

For weeks after the initial change catastrophe, I knew Max as the kid who ate change. He had been reduced to something little more than a quirk to me and inside that did not feel right. As his teacher I felt a responsibility to know what was underneath Max's willingness to allow himself to be the butt of other children's jokes. I wanted to know more about him; I *needed* to know more about him. I went to Tara Wyland with my concerns about Max. She said she would do some investigating into his situation and get back to me. What she would find was heartbreaking. Max had been separated from his mother at a very early age. Tara and I could not get specific information as to the reason for the removal of Max and his brother from their mother's care. All we needed to know was that Max's mother was not allowed access to any of her children until they were 18. I couldn't imagine a mother doing something so horrible that the state would take her children away and never return them. I was sick inside trying to grapple with what she could have done to her own flesh and blood to make her unfit to care for them. I had heard of the kind of abuse children suffered at the hands of unfit parents, but only from case studies in textbooks. I had never seen the object of such abuse, but now one was sitting in my class each day. I didn't want to imagine what Max had suffered as a young boy, I couldn't think of him being hurt in any way. Max was no longer the boy who ate change. He was not a mini freak show. Max was a boy who had been hurt or endangered in an unknown way by his own mother. Something gave way in me then. I was angry with Max's mother for hurting him, and I didn't even know the full story. All I needed to know was that I never wanted Max to feel hurt in any way. I imagined he had experienced enough of it in his short life. I didn't want him to be the object of dares from his peers or jokes and jeers in the hallways. I wanted to protect Max.

One day in class, I sat Max down and explained to him why I didn't want him to eat coins anymore. He genuinely did not understand my concern. Perhaps he had not, in his own life, been surrounded by people who cared enough to be concerned about him. I told him about the germs that he could be ingesting and what the money could do to his stomach. I told him that I didn't want him to get sick and I didn't want him to hurt himself. I don't think he got it at first, he laughed it off and said the only reason he ate the money was because he could; it was something he could do that others could not, so he did it. He conceded defeat and dropped the subject but I knew I would not. I would make it my goal to make sure Max did not put himself in danger in a way that could be even remotely similar to the way I imagined his mother already had. I felt a need to protect him because it seemed to me that the one person who should have protected him above all else had failed him. I would not.

When I first started teaching I told my friends and family that the best kind of birth control was spending 5 days a week with 150 teenagers. I had never been what I considered the mothering type. When my mother told me she longed for at least one grandchild, my reply was always that I was not good with living things, or that I had a hard enough time taking care of myself. After teaching for only a few months, I was certain that my children at school were enough for me. I could never imagine being a mother; it was not something that was in me. My students even began to joke with me, asking me when I was going to have kids, knowing that my reply would always be a resounding, "Never!" I was too independent to care for someone else all the time. I suppose I was too selfish to think of always putting someone else first. I decided that I wasn't going to be the kind of wife who had kids and took them to the park and packed them lunches. I never saw those kinds of mothers negatively. Those mothers can be a child's dream. The image just wasn't me. I was a feminist for god's sake. Feminists don't have mothering instincts. Aren't feminists cold, rigid, loveless beings looking only to destroy the male machine in modern day America? No. Max taught me that feminists can be quite the opposite.

One day Max asked me if I had kids. I told him that I did not and his reply was that I should one day have kids. I was taken aback by such a comment and told him I didn't think I would be a very good mom. He paused for a moment and said, "I think you would be a good mom." I sat back in my chair and asked him plainly, how he knew I would be a good mom. Without a second thought, Max looked me in the eyes and said, "Because if I could have you as my mom, I would."

My eyes began to sting and I tried to hold onto my emotion, though after only a few seconds, tears assaulted my face. I knew what Max had been through as a child. I knew that he associated pain and betrayal with his own mother. Max needed someone to take care of him after all he had been through in his life. He needed someone to love him and make his life a safe and happy one. Of all the people in the world, he would choose me as a mom if he could. Max saw me as a woman who was capable of creating a safe and loving place for him. He would choose me to take him to the park and pack his lunch. I was profoundly moved and stunned at the same time. I had never seen myself as a person who could take care of someone else; who could give of themselves enough to put someone else first. But Max saw me as that kind of person. And while we can't choose our parents, if he could, he would choose me. At that moment, my heart melted and when I looked into Max's eyes, I knew that if I could be his mom, I would.

Ever since that day Max and I have spent a lot of time together. He started sitting in the desk I keep next to my own in the classroom. Usually, this space is reserved for those who do not succeed in general population, and need a tighter reign held on them. Max did not see the desk next to the teacher as a punishment. The first time he sat there, he did so on his own accord. I noticed the change in Max gradually. I noticed that he began picking up papers for me, and passing back quizzes and homework assignments without being asked. He was gravitating more and more towards me. He began eating his lunch quickly in the cafeteria and leaving lunch early to come up to my classroom and spend the remainder of the period there. When he finished his work in study hall, or sometimes before he finished it, Max came to see me. He found his safe place, the place that made him feel at home, and it was in my classroom. Now, he pulls up a chair next to me when I am sitting at my desk. When I can I work on his homework with him, and when I am busy, he just sits next to me. Max needs someone that he feels safe with and I am thrilled to be that person for him. We even have a handshake. It is ours alone, a way to let the other know we care. And when I forget the handshake before I leave him, he holds out his hand as a reminder. And when he forgets, I remind him, and he always comes back.

A relationship like the one Max and I share is difficult to explain. Some of my students have asked me why Max is allowed to come into my room whenever he wants to. They think it is strange that he wants to spend time with one of his teachers. I try to give them an answer they can grasp without making Max too much of a "special case." The truth is, Max *is* special, and he needs more attention than some of my other students need. He needs time and attention, the kind most students get at home. Does spending extra time with Max mean that I am playing favorites? To some, it might. To me, it means that I am doing my job. My job is to educate students, and students are people. If I ignore the person that exists within each of my students I am not doing my job. There are some students that have barriers that prevent them from achieving their optimum learning potential. If a child is not well fed, they cannot focus on math for example. But sometimes, children have hunger that is not physical. Max's hunger is for someone who cares about him, someone he can latch on to, someone who will nurture him a little. If I ignore that need, that hunger, I am not reaching Max the person, therefore I cannot reach Max the student. My relationship with Max has never been something I have to think about and engage in consciously. My relationship with Max is an unconscious response to my own humanity. I cannot help caring about him, because he needs it. More than that, maybe I needed to care about someone that way.

Max is the only person who has ever made me think I could have a child; a thought I would have never entertained before he came into my life. I care about Max the way I think I would care about my own child. I love him unconditionally, with all of his faults and missteps, and I want only positive experiences for him. Max made me realize that I am more caring than I thought I ever could be. He showed me my own heart. Are students supposed to do that? Are students supposed to teach us about ourselves? My textbooks said no, but Max taught me otherwise. He has shown me the most human side of myself as a person, and as an educator. He melted the walls I had that blocked humanity out because it scared me too much, or because it wasn't "professional." I sometimes think about what it would be like if I was Max's mom. I think about how I would try to undo all that has been done to him. I wonder if he will ever know what he has done for me, and I doubt he will. Long after he has left my classroom, I will care for him, the way a mother is supposed to care for her child; the way his own mother could not.

*

Natalie's mom used to lock the cupboards in her kitchen so she couldn't eat just anything when she got home from school. Her mom would leave fruit on the table for Natalie and her sister because she did not want them to get fat. I had never heard a story like Natalie's. When Natalie told me that story I tired to imagine what that would feel like. I looked down at myself and wondered what her mother would think of me. I probably wouldn't have even gotten the fruit. Listening to Natalie, I felt ashamed of my own body and no one had ever locked the cupboards on me. Upon hearing the story, I instantly understood Natalie a bit more than I had before she told it. Natalie was a very insecure young woman when I met her. She was beautiful and sweet but very timid and quite withdrawn. I always wondered why she didn't have more confidence and why she didn't think more of herself. I understood when I closed my eyes and envisioned a young girl coming home from school to locked cupboards for fear that she would put on a little weight. She locked part of herself inside just like her mom had locked the food in the cupboards. I have tried to pull Natalie out of the shell she hides in; afraid to let any one see her, afraid they might not approve. Today Natalie is a little different than she was when I first met her. Her head is slightly higher when she walks down the hall than it was two or three years ago. But when I tell her she looks nice, she smiles shyly and hits me on the shoulder saying, "No I don't." I still worry about her sometimes.

"Help."

When I met Sabrina, she terrified me. Sabrina burst into my room with black hair and black clothes, donning chains and a spiked dog collar around her neck. Sabrina's attitude was even darker than the makeup around her eyes. There was no way I could fool or scare her. Sabrina saw through the tough image I tried to portray. I had been taught in my education classes that I had to be firm in order to prevent myself from being the proverbial doormat for teens. I had to make sure my students knew who the boss was and show them that I was a force to be reckoned with. I was good at the act too, even impressing myself. I have, since my first days of teaching, become infamous to students for my flare for sarcasm and rigidity, but Sabrina saw through the act before any of the other students did. She wore it on her face. When I looked at Sabrina, her eyes said, "Lady, you do not scare or fool me." Sabrina was the kind of kid I assumed could scare any teacher. She was rough. Her mouth was even louder than her attitude. She was not afraid to tell anyone what she thought. How was I supposed to handle a kid who could handle me? She stumped me, but I knew I had to figure out a way to create a relationship with her. Without a rapport with Sabrina, I would get nowhere. She was not the type of student who listened and followed, simply because it was her role as a student. She did not follow norms set up by others. I had to give Sabrina a reason to trust me, respect me, and listen to me, or she would do none of those things. She never said that, but I knew.

I had to think quickly with Sabrina. I had to know what to do and be sure of it, or I would fail and I would lose her. So, I came up with the only thing I knew how to do. I had to let Sabrina be herself. I had to step back, and just let her be. In the beginning, my course of action caused serious disruption. Sabrina didn't see my plan right away. She seemingly had free reign of my classroom. I saw fear in the eyes of the other students when Sabrina went on one of her rants. There were moments when I thought I would have to go back on my silent vow to respect Sabrina enough to let her be herself with no restraints. When she spoke quickly and curtly, expressing her very loud opinions on any topic (including some of my assignments), I didn't chide her or chastise her. I let her talk. At first, she wanted to see how far she could push me, but I didn't push back. I got out of her way. And eventually she realized that I was listening. I knew I couldn't make Sabrina be someone she wasn't. She was never going to be the kind of student who walked in each day and quietly sat down at her desk ready and eager to learn whatever I was teaching. Knowing that, I didn't try to change her. I didn't try to make Sabrina fit into a mold of every teacher's dream pupil. I realized that if she would not change for me, I would alter my own style for her. After all, I was the adult in the situation. I could adapt, and I would.

After a while, I grew braver than I had been when Sabrina walked into my class the first day. So when Sabrina challenged me, I challenged her right back. When she sassed me, I sassed her right back. I let her know that I would not let her run me, but I also would not try to run her. And we developed a mutual respect for one another. I respected the fact that Sabrina didn't take any shit, and I think she respected the fact that I didn't take hers. We had a good working relationship, until one day when everything changed. Sabrina stayed late after class and asked to talk to me. I thought with certainty that I had pissed her off and she was there to let me know it. But what happened when she sat down in a desk across from me was something I could never have prepared myself for. She spoke first.

"You have to promise me that you won't tell anyone what I am about to tell you." She had no idea that there are some promises teachers can't make, and for a moment, I forgot that fundamental truth.

"Okay, I promise."

I never should have made that promise. I knew that if Sabrina was in any kind of danger I would have to tell someone, I was bound by law to do so. But before I could retract the promise I wrongfully made, she rolled up the sleeves on her shirt and laid her arms out in front of me. The slashes on her arms were red and puffy. Her flesh was torn in at least ten places. Some of the marks looked fresh while others wore the scabs of age. I knew instantly, by the clean nature of the bloodied trails, that they were made with a razor, and that they were intentional. I stared into the marks on Sabrina's arms, hypnotized and unable to look away from that horror. The lump in my throat choked me and the air in my lungs became scarce. My heart beat in my ears loudly as I scrolled trough all of my training, scanning my memory for the chapter on students who self mutilate. There was no such chapter. No one told me what to do when a young woman came to me and showed me that she had been cutting herself. Then something pierced the air. I was snapped back into the reality that there was a girl in front of me who was obviously scared and feeling quite alone. They were the softest, gentlest words I had ever heard Sabrina utter, but they rang in my ears more loudly than her greatest tirade. Her words chilled me to the core, piercing my thoughts, my ears, and my heart.

"Help me."

I don't remember now what I said to her initially. I only remember looking for words and not finding the right ones. I was in shock. I didn't know what to say and I certainly didn't know what to do. In front of me sat a fifteen-year-old girl who had been cutting herself. I didn't know why and I didn't know how someone could actually take a blade to skin and let it penetrate. What could be so bad in Sabrina's life that she was hurting herself? What was happening at home? What was happening in her head? The thought of what could have caused Sabrina's cutting scared me almost as much as not knowing what to do as she sat there in front of me, waiting for me to speak. My resilience against my own tears fell apart when she told me that she couldn't stop, though she wanted to, and she didn't know what to do. I told her I would have to tell her guidance counselor what she had been doing to herself, because he was trained to help her while I was not. I spent much of the conversation talking her into letting me talk to her counselor. At first, she refused, and I desperately did not want to betray her confidence even though I had to if it came to that. I had to convince her to give me permission to talk to him, though I knew I would have to tell him with or without that permission. I cursed myself in my head for promising her I wouldn't tell anyone. I should have known better. I knew that legally I had to tell someone that one of my students was in danger of seriously hurting herself. I didn't want to betray her but aside from the fact that it would have been illegal for me to keep quiet, keeping quiet would have let her down even more. If she did not give me permission to tell her counselor I knew I would lose her, and that all the work I had done to reach her would have been for nothing. I knew that a betrayal on my part would not be forgiven and Sabrina and I would regress back to the time when she saw us as two people on opposite sides working against one another instead of together. But I also knew that I would rather have her alive hating me, than carry her secret to her funeral.

Eventually I was able to make Sabrina understand that she had to talk to her counselor. I also made her understand that legally I had to tell him what she told me. I told her I would do anything I could to help her and that she could talk to me any time. She told me that things were bad at home. She couldn't talk to her mom or her dad; she didn't think any one understood her. She didn't think any one was listening. She was a teenager. She had doubts and fears and demons locked within her that she didn't know how to deal with. She was hurting inside and that hurt was manifesting itself on the outside. She talked and I listened. The way she looked at me while she was talking made me painfully aware that she had never been sure anyone was listening until then. Not only was I listening to her, I was hearing her. There was more to what she spoke of than her words, there was a history of pain and confusion, a history of anger that had not been dealt with. Sabrina needed someone to help her. She needed much more help than I was able to give. But the moments we spent together in my classroom were a start. Though I could not help her the way I knew she needed, I could at least let her know that there are people out there who listen. Sabrina thought no one would ever be willing to listen, but I was. That made her realize that there are people in the world who care.

By the time she left my room she was ready to talk to her counselor. I was no longer trying to hide my tears as Sabrina walked out my door. The tears turned to sobs as soon as I was alone in my classroom. After a few moments, when enough time for Sabrina to get to her next class had passed, I ran through the halls looking for her counselor, hoping to get to him in time to call her down to his office. I was sick inside. I wanted so desperately to help Sabrina though I knew the best I could do was listen to her, and I didn't know if that was enough. Finally, breathless, I found Sabrina's counselor. He was not alarmed by the news I delivered to him. He told me she had been in and out of therapy since she was a young girl. She was the typical troubled youth. Typical troubled youth? What did that mean? There was nothing typical about Sabrina to me. I resented him for brushing her case off so casually. Though I knew he would do what he was trained to do for her, following the proper channels to make sure she didn't hurt herself, I wanted him to show me some emotion. I wanted Sabrina to be more real to him, like she was to me. I didn't want her to be just another teenager with problems. She was special and fragile on the inside of a very rough exterior. She was in trouble. I cared about Sabrina and I was worried about her. I knew Sabrina's counselor had probably seen a hundred cases like Sabrina, maybe even worse. But she wasn't a case in my mind. I hadn't seen anything like what she showed me on her arms, and it affected me, I wasn't numb to it yet, and had no idea how I ever would be.

Sabrina got the help she needed to understand and stop her cutting. I learned through that moment of terror with Sabrina that I will never be the kind of teacher who can leave my work at school. For days after Sabrina showed me her arms I went home with the sick feeling that I might not see her again when I got to school the next day. I was terrified that hurting herself would stop being enough for her and she would take her own life. I couldn't get her out of my head. I had heard many times that teaching is so difficult partly because if you let it, it will eat at you. I couldn't help but allow my fear for Sabrina and her safety to eat at me. I could not leave her at school. Sabrina followed me home each and every night. She lingered with me all the time. Eventually I began to trust that she would be okay, that her therapy was working. But learning about the ways teaching can haunt you was difficult for me. It was a lesson learned the hard way.

Since she initially brought me into her confidence, Sabrina and I have only become closer. She still maintains her hard as nails image though I know a different side of her. I have her brother in class now and I have watched how protective of him she is. She takes care of him, even though she pretends to hate him, as all teenage siblings do. She came into my room not too long ago and told me that her mom walked out on her family. One day, Sabrina's mom just picked up and walked out, leaving the kids with their father. Sabrina took on two jobs to help pay the bills. She said her plans to go to college had been put on hold since most of her college money would be spent on groceries and electric bills. Her face was stoic the day she came into my room to tell me the news. She was the picture of what growing up too fast must look like. She was the image of having too much responsibility for someone who inside was still only a little girl. Sabrina's story is one that chills me to the bone. Her aunt and her brother are the only family members she says she can count on. She is angry with her mom for leaving and angry with her dad for drinking most of her youth away. She has had little time to be a kid, something I can tell she desperately needs.

Not long after Sabrina's mom left home, she and I were in a play together. For the first time since I met her, I got to see her be passionate about something. I saw excitement in her face at the thought that she was a part of something bigger than she was, something bigger than most teens are able to even comprehend. Sabrina always tried to make everyone think she cared about nothing but herself. But I saw something different in her early on in our relationship. I have seen her give of her time for charity and for her family. I have seen her put herself out for people who do not always return the favor. I learned, through knowing Sabrina, that looking beyond someone's exterior is one of the most important parts of being a teacher. I saw beyond Sabrina's chains, black clothes, and the dark makeup that hides her eyes. I saw beyond the scars and cuts on her arms. I saw the person in Sabrina; a person I admire for what she has been through and what she continues to struggle through. Sabrina exists against odds that have been stacked against her. Sabrina's story has tortured me, tried me, and has made me smile. She has trusted me with her demons and fears, and I feel I have been given the gift of knowing who she really is. She is a testament to courage and resilience. I am changed because of Sabrina, because I know that things can always be worse than you think. I also know, because of her, that we as individuals can either let ourselves be beaten, or we can fight. Sabrina is a fighter.

*

When I think about all the people who must think I am crazy or that I go too far trying to teach my students how to be good people and how to respect and accept those around them, I remember the time a student asked me the following question. Hearing a student speak these words made me certain that more of us should work towards giving students a sense of humanity as well as a sense of good grammar and punctuation.

"If we didn't have any black kids in our school, would we have to come to school on Martin Luther King Day?"

Students need more than one may think.

Bringing Winds of Change

Vanessa and Adrian are changing the world. I wonder sometimes if they understand how rare they are, or how commendable their work is. I came to know these two spectacular women in my second year of teaching. Patrick came to my room one day and asked me to be in a play called *The Vagina Monologues*. I had heard of the play before, in college, and had read the book by Eve Ensler. I knew the play to be an intense look at female sexuality and emotion but beyond that, I knew very little. Patrick told me that Vanessa and Adrian came to know the play and wrote to the author to get permission to produce it as a part of the annual V-Day celebration. I had no idea what V-Day was, but have come into my own awareness because of Vanessa and Adrian. V-Day is Valentines Day. However, the V-Day organization started calling Valentines Day "V-Day" until violence against women around the world is stopped. Each year, during the month of February, V-Day campaigns across the world put on performances of *The Vagina Monologues* to raise money to stop violence against women. Usually performances of the Monologues are found on college campuses, although some high schools across the country have been known to put on performances of the piece. Our high school, however, would not affiliate itself with the play. The powers that be had a problem with the word "vagina". I can't even say that now with a straight face. I can't imagine not lending support to a worthy cause because its title uses the biologically correct word for female genitalia. It is maddening to me as a woman, as a feminist, and as an educator. But Vanessa and Adrian did not waste time getting angry about the fact that the school wouldn't support the play, they decided to do it anyway.

Vanessa and Adrian spearheaded a kind of underground performance of *The Vagina Monologues*, complete with advertisements for the play in the stalls of the school bathrooms. I was thrilled to have been asked to be a part of it.

61

Patrick was the only male involved in the campaign and decided to ask me to join the ranks. He knew me well enough to know that I would love to be a part of something so much bigger than me. He was right. As a part of the V-Day campaign Vanessa and Adrian put together, I would read one of the monologues in a small performance at a community center near the school. Since we couldn't advertise for the play at school, publicly at least, the students involved went to the town for support. Vanessa and Adrian worked tirelessly to seek out financial sponsors, people willing to donate time or equipment, and patrons to come to the performance. They were unbelievable. Two young women, who had little time to spare, gave of their own time and money to produce the play, which would benefit a local battered women's shelter. I watched Vanessa and Adrian in awe of what they were doing. As a high school teenager I would never have thought to devote so much of myself to the greater good of anyone. While many of their peers buckled under the pressures of school alone, Vanessa and Adrian took on the responsibility of rigorous honors courses, various clubs, and the task of trying to make the world a better place for women. They were two young women who found a cause they cared about and threw themselves into that cause. It was beautiful to watch and to be a part of.

We met one night a week to discuss progress made with the fundraising aspect of the V-Day campaign and to rehearse the play. Each time we met, Vanessa and Adrian had come up with more ways to make money for the shelter. They were tireless in their efforts to make a difference in their own small way. They inspired the other students and adults in the campaign into action, putting up flyers and making phone calls. It was an exciting time to be a woman and an exciting time to be a teacher. There is something to be said for watching students outside of the classroom. To see students as people who have passion and life in them that so many people miss is a gift. Vanessa and Adrian energized all of us as we worked on the play. When the time finally came for the production of *The Vagina Monologues*, it was a success. None of the people involved were professional actors, just women (and Patrick) who cared about stopping the violence that women all over the world face. But that amazing night, everyone who spoke was a bright star, burning with the fire that Vanessa and Adrian ignited. Being a part of the play was an incredible high. I felt empowered and alive in a way I had never known. The night was beautiful and powerful. I remember looking out at the audience during my monologue. A woman in the audience was crying as I spoke about the miracle of childbirth. I reached out and touched her with words that inspired me even as I read them. After the play, we all gathered in a small room offstage and couldn't stop cheering and laughing and hugging one another. We celebrated a victory. We knew that by raising enough money to help even one woman escape abuse, we were victorious. There was courage and unity in the air. It came from Vanessa and Adrian. They showed everyone involved with the V-Day campaign that even the smallest ripples can turn into waves.

I was thrilled when Vanessa and Adrian asked me to take part in the play for a second year. They were even more dedicated than they had been the year before. I watched all over again the drive and passion they both had for the pursuit of a world without violence against women. The second time around, part of the money raised would go to Juarez, Mexico where women have been disappearing from factories and turning up raped and murdered while no one has been prosecuted for the crimes. Vanessa and Adrian produced the play with even more enthusiasm than they had the year before. They were two women who could see the bigger picture. They showed that picture to me. No matter how old you are you can make a difference. No matter how small you may think you are you can save the life of someone you don't even know. Those are only two of the lessons I took away from my time with Vanessa and Adrian. At our most recent performance I sat on stage while Sabrina (yes, that Sabrina) performed her monologue and thought to myself that if I could, by being a part of the play, help even one woman sleep without fear, I would be making a difference. Vanessa and Adrian made me see that as a possibility. They showed me that I could be a part of something that touches lives selflessly. They helped me help others. Vanessa and Adrian are angels to women who have lived in fear for too long or who have been beaten too many times. They are my angels too. They gave all of us the chance to know that even a few people can make a difference in the world. I feel better knowing that they are on my side, that they would help me if I needed it. They don't ask for praise or accolade, simply a safe place for women in this world. I never knew there would be students like Vanessa and Adrian in my school, or in any school for that matter. All too often we, as teachers and as people, believe what I now realize is a myth, that all teenagers are apathetic, that they only care about themselves. Too many people tend to think that teenagers want to go out with their friends, party, and see what they can get away with. People don't understand that there are teenagers out there, maybe in the schools where we teach, or in the neighborhoods where we live, who are passionate about the world around them. There are young people who want to make the world better for themselves and for people they have never even met. I didn't go to school with people like Vanessa and Adrian, and thus I fell victim to believing that they weren't out there somewhere. But as a teacher I found them, I found two women who cared more about others in some circumstances than they cared about what was going on after school or on Friday night after the football game. I am happy to have met Vanessa and

Adrian as an educator, because I am able to appreciate them more than I would have as a student. Many of the students in their own school don't understand and appreciate the work these women do. As an educator, I am able to see them as warriors in a fight that for a long time had no name and no face to go with it. I am able to applaud them for the fact that they give to people who need it, without a desire for thanks or praise. Most of all, at any stage of my life I am happy to know two warriors in the fight to stop violence against women. I am a warrior next to them, fighting alongside them, letting them lead me into battle. Vanessa and Adrian are women I admire and am proud to know.

*

Students should be asked to challenge themselves, not only academically, but where their beliefs, ideas, and prejudices lie…

During a debate on gay marriage, when a student tried to claim that homosexuality was not natural, his defense was:

"Of course homosexuality isn't natural. Frogs aren't gay."

To which I responded…

"How do you know? Have you talked to a frog lately?"

Anna

    Since the beginning of this journey, I have tried to figure out how to explain my relationship with Anna and it has been a daunting task. Anna is the student to whom I am the closest. I have known Anna since day one. She was in my second period Honors class, my first year of teaching. She made herself known to me on the second day of class. On the first day I had given the class a three-fold assignment, covering their books being one of the tasks. During the second class with my Honors students, I went through the roster one by one and gave the students a minus, a check, or a check-plus, depending on how many of the three tasks they had completed. When I got to Anna, she had only completed two of the tasks. When she realized that she was getting a less than perfect mark in my grade book, she had what I can only call a breakdown right there in my class. Her eyes grew to the size of golf balls and she sat straight up in her chair. She tried to speak, but she was muttering like a crazy person and none of it was quite comprehensible. She rocked back and forth a bit in her chair and stared straight into my eyes, a bead of sweat forming on her brow. She was panic-stricken and I thought for a moment that I was going to have to get a paper bag for her to breathe into. I was instantly aware that Anna would settle for nothing less than perfection in my class, and for that matter, anywhere. She was willing, on that second day, (once she got her composure) to speak what she felt and not back down. She made an impression right away. I told the story of Anna and the check in my grade book as my first official story from teaching. It wasn't something enormous or life altering, but it was a moment that stood out to me. It was a moment that defined one of my students for me. That moment, however insignificant it may seem now or may have seemed then, was my first lesson on Anna. I remember laughing that day, laughing at Anna's reaction to her check in the grade book, but inside I was laughing for another reason. I was laughing because I could see some of my high school self reflected in her. I could see my own high-strung nature reflected back at me in another person. I knew how she felt when she found out she was only getting a check when she expected to get a check-plus. I knew what it felt like to be so intense and so focused on success that anything short of it seems like impossibility. To this day, Anna swears that I told her she would only need two of the tasks completed for day two of my class. Knowing what I know about her now, I have often wondered if she is right, and if the incident that started our relationship was a mix-up on my part. Three years after the grade book incident, Anna is sure that if I truly expected more of her, she would have delivered. I would have done the same thing for any of my teachers. It is a unique experience to find a piece of yourself in someone else, especially when that someone else is a student and you are the teacher. Thus started my relationship with Anna; a simple recognition of the me that I saw in her.

Early on in my career as an educator, Anna and I gravitated toward one another. Since then, I have had some time to realize why we fit together so well. When I was at school I didn't feel like I belonged there. During my first year of teaching I never felt like I knew enough or was good enough to be a teacher. I felt like I was playing a part that I wasn't cut out for. I felt a bit like a fish must feel when snatched from its water. I tried to breath but the air was heavy and it didn't come through my gills no matter how hard I tried. All of my colleagues were more professional than I was, more well-read, better at what I was supposed to do than I was. While they became my friends, I was still nervous around them, fearing that I would never be good enough for them to call me equal. Anna made some of the fear and uneasiness drift away for me. Anna made me feel like I fit in my own skin. She made me feel like it was okay for me to just be who I was and not worry about what the people around me would say or think about me. She made me realize that as long as I was true to myself, I was right. I learned those lessons by watching Anna, watching her slash the high school "norm" to pieces and be her own person, no matter what anyone thought or said. I got along with Anna the way I got along with my childhood friends, with unspoken understanding. I didn't think of her as a student for long. I remember talking about her to my family and friends and they all asked me, "Are you talking about one of your students?" I asked myself the same thing. It was clear to everyone that I didn't think of Anna as a student though I taught her every day. She listened and did her work and was one of my most dedicated pupils, but she was never just one of my students. The thing about Anna was not her work ethic or her keen wit. The thing about Anna was that she never seemed to belong in my class with the other students. She was what I considered to be an old soul. She had grown-up ideas and ways. She was the spitting image of a thirty-year-old trapped in a fourteen-year-old body.

Anna and I continue to joke about the fact that her age as well as her mindset and attitude don't match. The first time I told her she was wiser than her age projected her to be, she said her mom had always told her the same thing. It was obvious to everyone around her. Perhaps that was why it was so easy for me to talk to Anna when she came into my room daily during her study hall. After all, what teacher wants to talk to students when they don't have to? What a silly notion. Isn't that what my education professors told me? Students are not friends they are students, nothing more. But Anna was different. Anna was more. She was more interesting, more intelligent, more outspoken, more witty than many of the people I had met in my lifetime. She was more mature than some people my own age or older. She was a being elevated beyond her age to some sort of heightened adulthood. There was always a conflict in my head though. I really liked Anna. I liked talking to her and being around her but in the back of my head I could always hear my professors reminding me that students and teachers cannot be friends. I could imagine my colleagues wondering why I was so close to one of my students. I could hear them in my head, talking about the rookie who wasn't able to draw the line. It was somehow different with Patrick. There was something in my head that could rationalize him; he needed to talk to someone, to be out to someone and that brought us together. But Anna did not have something that set her apart from everyone else that way. I didn't think she needed me. She was just someone I genuinely enjoyed; the way you meet someone over drinks and think, "Wow, we could be great friends."

While Anna was in my class I tried to consider her a student first. I was aware that it was my job to educate those who came through my door. I was smart enough to know that a line had to be drawn, no matter how difficult it was to stay on one side of that line. When she left my class though it was easy to see Anna as a friend. She made going to school each day easier. We talked about everything. If I had a bad day, I could tell her about it. I could tell her that I screwed up a lesson or misspoke during a lecture. She would reassure me by saying most of the kids probably didn't notice. Sometimes that made me feel better and sometimes I wondered if she knew something I didn't, that no one was listening to me in the first place. Either way, she made me feel better during the rough spots in my day. We talked about her friends and why she didn't want to drink or have sex like some of the other kids were already doing. We talked about where she wanted to go to college and why it had been such a big deal when she didn't get a check-plus in my grade book on her second day in class. She was a bright spot in a job that I sometimes feared would get the best of me. We became close quickly, and in a way that is difficult to trace. All of a sudden Anna was there, more than an occupant in a class, but a friend, someone I needed around to laugh with and talk to. She drifted in quickly and quietly, unseen but then realized as a fixture. Her presence was normal and natural to me. And I stopped trying to explain to people why Anna and I had the relationship we did, not only because it was too difficult, but because it was too special. Anna became someone very important to me. At times though, there was a part of me that still worried. I worried that I had done Anna an injustice by being more of a friend than an influence to her. Perhaps my professors had been right. You can't have it both ways. You can't be teacher and friend because the two will be in constant conflict. But one day Anna quelled my worry.

Sometimes in teaching, it can feel like the bad days outweigh the good days. However, there are some circumstances when an intensely bad day can lead to something wonderful. One of my worst days came toward the middle of my second year of teaching. I had two sophomore classes in my schedule, a grade I had not mastered. After teaching grades 9-12 I have decided that sophomores are the most challenging. They are coming into their own and they have a lot to prove. They need to show everyone around them that they aren't the babies of the school. They need to fight for a place and discover their own sense of themselves. For those reasons, I have always found sophomores difficult to control. Some days can be better than others but the bad days with sophomores can be overwhelming. Toward the middle of my second year there was a day when I felt like I was talking to walls instead of sophomores; no one cared what I had to say and I thought the whole class would be better off if I just jumped out the window. At least they would pay attention to me crashing into the shrubbery below my classroom window. By the end of one of my sophomore classes I felt beaten and bruised. I didn't know if I could even come in the next day, or any day after that. I was at my wits end. I didn't think I could even finish out the day. I had been berated all day about my lessons and my homework, interrogated repeatedly by students who demanded to know why they had to read at all in English class. It was a day that made me question my decision to become an educator. I couldn't understand how any student in any high school in America could actually question reading and writing as part of an English curriculum. How could they not understand that they had to learn something in school? How could they keep asking, "Do we have to do this?" What was I doing wrong? Anna was in and out of my room all day, by now she was keeping some of her books on a shelf in my room instead of in her locker. She asked me if I wanted her to take care of the situation. Before

I could even answer, she looked at the class and asked them how they could be so disrespectful.

"This lady is not like other teachers here. Don't you realize that you are lucky to have her? Maybe you should all just shut up and listen to her."

She turned toward me after she addressed the class and smiled sweetly, victoriously, and then walked out of the room. A student had just fought one of my battles for me. Anna stood up in front of a class of her peers and told them off on my behalf because she saw in my face that I was on the edge. The class was silent for the remainder of the period and when the bell rang I was glad to see them leave. I needed a break.

The next day, returning to school was unbearable. When I walked in and was hit by the familiar smell of heavy perfume and stale sweat, packed lunches and morning coffee, I was angry with myself for not pulling the covers up to my eyes when I woke up and calling in sick. I went to the lounge to make copies, going through the motions, all the while thinking I was an absolute failure at my job, wondering how long it would take for the administration to find out and ask me to clean out my room and leave. The hum of the copy machine lulled me into a state of total despair. I feared I would be unable to face any of the students who had made the day before such a disaster. But maybe it wasn't their fault at all. Maybe it was my fault, for not knowing enough, not being strong enough, not having enough discipline. I entertained the thought that this day would be better, had to be better than the one before. Then the copier jammed, and I was sure my hope for a better day was nothing but fancy. The halls were filling with students by the time I left the lounge and I wished I could disappear. Dodging backpacks and high fives, wincing against the screamed morning greetings of girls who hadn't seen each other since the day before, I was certain I should walk past my own classroom and call it a day. I would be no good to anyone on a day that felt doomed before it even began. But when I approached my room something propelled me inside. Guilt perhaps? Lack of clarity? Instinct? Whatever it was that took over, I opened the door and went into my room. Crossing the floor to my desk, arms warmed by fresh copies, I saw something sitting on top of the papers that cluttered my workspace. Amidst the neglected assignments and blank attendance sheets lay a loaf of bread, that from the smell I could tell was homemade, and an envelope with my name on it. It wasn't a holiday. It wasn't my birthday. It wasn't even a good day. I looked around my room for a student who may have seen someone come in and drop off a gift, but I was alone. After laying down my copies, I fell into my chair, opened the envelope and read.

Ms. Gregor –

Where do I begin? You have been a great teacher this year and I have learned an incredible amount from you. To me, being a great teacher is such an important thing. But not only are you a great teacher, you are a wonderful person as well. I know that anytime I need someone to talk to, or someone to just listen, that you will be there. I really do not know what I would have done without you this year. It has been such a year of growth for me, and I feel you contributed so much toward that. I don't think I would be able to get through high school without someone like you. You are a wonderful teacher and mentor. You are the perfect example for me to follow. Thank you for a great year. You are a true inspiration of what a true teacher is.

The card was from Anna. I sat in the quiet of my classroom and I thought about what Anna wrote. I had affected her. I had worried that allowing myself to like her as a person had made me an ineffective mentor in her life, a failure as an educator where she was concerned. But I was wrong. I had done something right with Anna. Not only had she become someone I valued in my life as a person, I was a person she valued in her life as an influence. It was the perfect combination. I hadn't expected Anna to see me as an influence in her life. She was the kind of student I thought of as perfect already, the kind of student that would learn from me but not really need me. I thought she would take care of everything herself because she was strong and smart and seemed to have it all together for herself. But she defied my expectations as our relationship defied what I had been taught was right and proper. So many of my professors were wrong. You can't decide before you know your students what kind of relationship you will have with them. Each student is different from any other person in the world, and they can change you in ways you won't expect or be ready for, and you can leave lasting marks on them as well. I didn't know Anna and I would need each other, but it turned out we did. I needed to be reminded that to someone, I was useful, I was important. I needed a student to yell at my class and tell them they didn't deserve me and then bake me homemade bread the way a mom would bake chocolate chip cookies to make up for a bad day at school. And Anna needed me too, as an influence, as a mentor, and as a friend, someone who would understand her, listen to her, and let her be herself. Anna taught me not to have so many rules in my head, so many conventional ideas about what my students would or should be, or even about what I would or should be to them. I couldn't know how I would handle a student until they come through my classroom door. I couldn't predict the good or bad days any more than I could prepare for them. I couldn't predict that a student would give me back my faith in myself. I couldn't predict that a student would quickly become a friend. I didn't know when I met her that Anna would become like a little sister to me, but she has. Is that wrong? No, it is just unconventional. And in teaching, convention is not always the best guide.

Through my relationship with her daughter, and the fact that she also works at the school, I have come to know Anna's mom. I remember the first time I met her. It was during conferences and I was standing outside my classroom waiting for my next appointment to arrive. A petite woman, with wavy blonde hair walked up to me wearing a warm, lovely smile. She donned a pair of jeans and a stylish leather jacket. I could barely believe she was a parent, on any college campus she would have passed for a co-ed. "You must be Ms. Gregor," she said holding out her hand to greet me. "I am Anna's mom and I just had to come and meet you." Becky was a breath of fresh air. She glowed with friendliness and talking to her was like talking to any of my oldest and dearest friends. She spoke of how she had heard so much about me and I shared that I, likewise, had heard a lot about her and the rest of Anna's family. I felt like I knew them already when I met Becky for the first time. Since our first meeting, Becky has become my friend as well. Hers is a face I enjoy seeing each day. She is kind and full of life, making it easy to see where Anna gets her disposition. When I heard that Becky's mother died I knew instantly I needed to go to the funeral home, for Anna and for her mother. They were two important women in my life and they lost an important woman in their own lives. I wanted to be there for them. When I got to the funeral home I made my way through a sea of people I did not recognize and found Anna sitting in the back of the room. "I can't believe you came" was her greeting, and as I hugged her I assured her that of course I would be there to lend support and condolence for her and for her mom. She told me her mom was on automatic pilot, taking the death of her own mother hard. Becky was staying strong for her father, her kids, everyone else, but I knew she must be in her own private agony. I left Anna to find her mom and when I did she hugged me long and hard. She thanked me for being there though it was not something I felt I had to do, something I had to be thanked for. Going to see Anna and her mom at such a difficult time was a natural occurrence, because I cared for them. After visiting them at the calling hours for the matriarch of their family, I received the following note from Becky.

Dear Kylie,

Thank you so much for everything you have done for Anna & myself these last few weeks. It was so nice of you to come to the showing. We were glad to see you.

And thanks for always being there for Anna. You are so special to her. I feel very blessed that she has you in her life. I hope she <u>always </u>will! Thanks again.

Love,

Becky

Since the funeral I have been to Anna's house for dinner with her family. I have been able to watch Anna with her dad, how he loves and protects his little girl without holding on too tightly, and how she respects and loves him back. I have sat around the dinner table with them and laughed at their stories while sharing my own. They are people who are cut from an original mold, one that cannot be duplicated. There is a depth to their family that is easily enviable. I remember sitting at the dinner table thinking about how warm they all were, how they were so easy to talk to and how it was so easy to feel that with them I was among my own family. That is what they have become to me, an extension of my own family. After dinner, while Anna cleaned up the dishes her mom thanked me for being there for Anna when her grandmother died. She told me that Anna needed someone to talk to and I had been that person for her. She said they were lucky to have me, when the whole night I was feeling that I was the lucky one, to find such wonderful, welcoming people and be brought into their home and into their hearts.

Becky helped answer a question that often lingered in my head because of my relationship with Anna and some of my other students. What do parents think when their child has an unconventional relationship with a teacher? Is it weird? Is it taboo? My own answer was yes, it can be. Relationships with students can be touchy. No matter how close I am to a student, like Anna, I always know in my mind that I am the adult and the student is the child. There is still a line in the sand, though I don't always think of it as a barrier. My relationships with my students have always come out of a genuine caring for them as people. I care about their education and their lives. I know my place. However, perhaps some of the most positive feedback I have ever gotten has been from parents. Anna's mom did not see my relationship with her daughter as negative, but wonderful. Not only that, Anna's mom and I developed a relationship of our own, out of our mutual caring for Anna and a mutual respect and enjoyment for one another. Becky's answer to what parents might think about me was a welcomed surprise. She was thankful for me and my place in Anna's life, and she welcomed me into her own life as well. I never thought that my job as an educator could make my family grow, but it has. In Anna and in Becky, I have found people I can no longer imagine my life without. They are people who have affected me deeply; people I will know and love for the rest of my life. I am thankful for them every day.

*

Mitch got his first B in my class. He called it the quarter of hell because we read *The Great Gatsby* and the symbolism in the novel seemed, at times, to both evade and haunt him. During the third quarter, when he saw his final grade I thought he was going to have a nervous breakdown. It was as if I told him he was going to lose a limb. There was a part of me that felt really bad for him, because I knew how much his grades meant to him. But, the educator in me knew that he earned a B and there was nothing I could do to change his grade, even if I wanted to, my code as a teacher would forbid it. I also knew that at some point in Mitch's life, he would get less than a perfect score. I thought it was good for him to get a B because he would learn to accept what he considered failure at an early age. When Mitch freaked out about his B, it prompted me to talk to all of my honors students about grades. I wanted them to know that not everyone gets all A's all the time. I wanted Mitch and the others to know that if they got a B in a class, or even a C, they weren't failures. I didn't want them to boil themselves down to just their grades. Part of learning is the experience itself, not just the grade slapped on a report card at the culmination of an assignment, unit, or grading period.

The truth is, Mitch is one of the best students I have ever had in class. He is bright and he is more capable than he realizes. I didn't want him to boil himself down to his grade in my class, because he was so much more than that grade. Some of the best discussions in Mitch's class came from his ideas. Mitch has plans to go to an Ivy League school and become a neurosurgeon. He plans on making those dreams come true and I don't doubt that he will. I don't think his B in my class will hurt him. I think it will help him. His mom once told me she thought it would help him too. Mitch's mom told me that I pushed him and that she saw that as quite valuable. Mitch puts too much emphasis on his grades, when he should dwell on the fact that he is smart and wildly talented. He just needs to relax. Mitch can do anything he wants to do, B or not.

Brandon

Brandon's family is from the Philippines. He holds onto his heritage with a tight grasp. He is proud of his brown skin and the tragedy, struggles, and joys that make up his family's history. Once Brandon told me the story of his grandmother. He said during a military coup she watched as members of her own family were dragged from her house and killed. That story, that moment in history, is one square of the patchwork that makes up Brandon's history. The blocks that build the foundation of Brandon's family are both horrific and inspiring. But far away from the land of his ancestors, a land some of them still inhabit, one that Brandon has not been able to visit for some time because of the threat of disease, Brandon's own story is the most inspiring to me. Brandon defies the stereotype of the typical American ninth grader. So many people, when I tell them that I teach freshmen, pity me because they assume all freshmen must be immature and hormone-crazed. I have seen smiles turn to fear when I answer the question, "What grade do you teach?" Sometimes, I pity myself as well, when I am trying to make fourteen-year-olds find a deep love for Shakespeare, or even trying to make them sit in their desks. Many of my freshmen students would rather play video games or listen to music than listen to me. Some of my freshmen don't even know I am there when I stand in front of them and ask them to take out a book. Some of them are too busy writing notes and drawing flowers, hearts, or skulls on their notebooks to care that they have a test the next day. But sometimes, someone like Brandon walks into the classroom, and everything you think about the typical ninth grader is crushed like a piece of chalk, just bits of dust on the floor.

Brandon greets me each day, formally, when he enters my room. He has never spoken disrespectfully to me in any circumstance. He extends the same courtesy to all of his teachers. He is polite; he asks, "May I use the restroom?"

When often that simple request is boiled down to a crass, "I have to pee." He does not interrupt me when I am speaking, and if others do, he quiets them with a look and a firm "Shhh!" Brandon asks me if I need help passing out papers, or if there is anything he can do for me when he finishes his work. When he has a feeling that I am having a bad day he says, "Is everything okay, Mrs. Whitmire?" When I am not feeling well, he apologizes and tells me to get some rest when I get home. He is the picture of good manners at all times and is a genuinely kind and caring individual.

Brandon is also an overachiever. He is obsessive compulsive about his work being done and about it being done to his teachers' exact specifications. I can't tell you how many times he has shown me his work before actually turning it in. At first, I thought Brandon was just one of those students who needed constant affirmation. I thought he needed me to tell him over and over again that his work was wonderful and that he had really good ideas. Some students have that need but Brandon is not one them. Brandon has a genuine desire to do well. It is part of the pride he takes in everything he does. Perhaps this comes from the fact that some of his family members live in a place with less opportunity than the country he now calls home. Perhaps he feels an obligation to do well, to use all of the tools he has at his disposal to make the most of himself. His drive stretches into everything he does. Brandon is also a football player who is constantly trying to make himself better. He goes to his coach and makes sure he is doing the best he can, not because he wants recognition for trying, but because he strives to be the best he can be for himself. Brandon is also quite politically savvy. He watches the world news each night with his father so he can keep up on issues that he cares about. He doesn't care that he won't be able to cast a ballot for four more years; he wants to know as much as he can about the world around him. Since it was an election year when I first met Brandon I saw the latter of his attributes very clearly, very quickly. He wanted to talk politics with me all the time. He wanted to voice his opinions and showcase some very impressive knowledge. Sometimes, he taught me about events that I was even unaware of, each day asking me if I watched the news the night before. I asked him once why, as such a young person, he cared so much. It wasn't even a question he could answer. He couldn't imagine not caring about his country, even as a young man who is not old enough to serve it or vote for the people or policies that will change it. Brandon is worldly and aware of news and events that other students his age or even older might think of as above their heads or a waste of time. I have friends who are not as aware, or do not care as much about the world as Brandon does. Needless to say, Brandon has impressed me from the day I met him.

It is one thing to see the strength, wits, or drive of a young man, but something altogether different to have him show you his heart. Brandon has a very big heart, and it is always in the right place. Brandon happened to be in my class at the same time as Max. Brandon witnessed the other kids teasing Max and daring him to perform acts that could hurt him. Watching this take place made Brandon angry, and one day he told me about it. Brandon came to me and asked to talk to me privately, saying it was very important. He waited until the other students in class had filed out the door with the sound of the bell. He retold accounts of the kids in class teasing Max and told me that he was concerned about it. Brandon told me that Max hadn't had a good life (which I already knew) and that he was trying to look out for Max. Brandon had told the other kids to knock it off or they would deal with an angry football player. But a threat wasn't enough. He wanted to make sure Max was okay. He wanted me to sit Max down and talk to him and let him know that he needed to start making good choices. Brandon cared so much it was heart-wrenching. In front of me was a young man who was willing to stick his neck out for a kid few people would even talk to. Brandon didn't care what people thought of him, he only cared about Max and about doing the right thing. Brandon wanted to be someone Max could trust and look up to. He wanted to protect Max. I was touched. I felt a little better knowing that Max had Brandon on his side. I felt good that I had Brandon on my side too. As a teacher it is hard to know all and see all though it is something all teachers go crazy trying to do. Brandon was, in some way, my eyes and ears when I wasn't able to see and hear everything going on. He was my ally. I knew Brandon could make a difference to a kid like Max who simply needed someone on his side.

Brandon has shown me the human side of a group too many people see as less than human. Brandon makes me proud to teach freshmen, and makes me realize I wouldn't trade them for anything in the world. People are people, no matter what age. The deepest parts of humanity exist in all of us. Some of us just don't show them all the time. Brandon is not afraid to show his humanity, even if it isn't cool, even if it makes him the guy who sticks up for someone no one else would stick up for. Brandon is the humanity in all of us that we should show more often.

*

There was no way I could have prepared for a student like Kyle. He has a spark that can ignite any class. His quirky sense of humor constantly has me wondering what he will do or say next. Kyle is the kind of student that can be easily distracted but always gets his work done. He is also the kind of student a teacher like me can have fun with, because he is as good at the sarcastic banter I love as anyone I have met in this field. The other day he told me our relationship was damaged because I wasn't letting him have fun in class. He said we would fight in a dual to the death. Then, he raised his shoulders towards his ears and gave me his famous smirk. I can't help but laugh at him. Once, we got into a water fight with the spray bottle I use to clean off my overhead projector. By the end of it we both looked like we had walked through a rainstorm. Perhaps my fondest memory of Kyle, though, is the time I asked him to help me hand out papers. To my request, he simply replied, "I am not your bitch." He had a point, and he didn't pass out the papers, he folded his arms across his chest and refused.

Silent Accolades

As a person and as a teacher, quiet people have always scared me. When I am in a room full of people, the silent ones make me the most nervous. I have been, since I was a child, somewhat worried about what people think of me. The quiet ones have always struck me as the thinkers. When a student sits in my room and doesn't say anything, that one student makes me more nervous than a roomful of kids who are willing to tell me exactly what they think of me. If someone tells you they think you are a jerk, at least you know they think you are a jerk. Likewise, if a person thinks you are wonderful, what is scary about hearing that? I would rather know what people think than fill myself with anxiety trying to piece together possibilities of what they could be saying about me in their heads. It's funny actually, in a roomful of students, the ones who want to stay under the radar, thus remaining quiet as mice, are the ones who make the largest impact on me as a teacher. Silent students do not go unnoticed; they make huge waves with their quiet demeanors, their avoidance of discussion or question. I have spent a great deal of time as a teacher wondering what the quiet kids in my class must be thinking when I stand at the front of the room.

When I teach, I am over the top; I am loud, I wave my arms, I pace, I sweat. At the end of class one day, after teaching one of my passions, Shakespeare, I realized that I had huge sweat marks on the back and underarms of the yellow shirt I was wearing. I joked with my students as they left class that I should not wear yellow during any discussion of Shakespeare. They laughed and didn't seem to mind the fact that their teacher was dripping wet with exhaustion and excitement. As the next class came in they looked at me with eyes that wondered, "What happened here?" When I love what I teach, which I usually do or I don't teach it, I cannot sit still. I cannot lecture from a stool or a chair.

85

I have to move. I have to feel what I am saying in my hands and my feet and make my students feel it too. The woman whose room borders mine to the north once came to the door after a class and said, "Wow, you must have been angry at your students today, I could hear you in my room." I laughed and explained to her that I was not angry, but excited by Shakespearean sonnets. I teach not only with my heart and soul, but also with my full voice and my body. Sometimes I sing, sometimes I make the students speak along with me. I am everywhere and everything all at once when I teach. I have found that the classroom is one place where I can be as me as I want to be and not worry. I had never felt comfortable around crowds until I became a teacher. But when I have a full audience, waiting to get their money's worth, I am ready to perform. My classroom is my stage. My critics are my students. If something doesn't work I can tell from their feedback and I can change it, alter the performance to make it a success. But the silent critics, how do you know what they think? How can you tell if your performance has been a success for them? Most of my kids respond quite well to my teaching style. I can read on the faces of my students that they are seeing something new in me, something unlike what they have experienced before, and that is what I want them to get out of my class; an experience they may never be able to duplicate. When I assign presentations to my students, I tell them I want them to move me, because that is what I try to do for them when I teach. I want them to remember what happens in my classroom years after they leave it. I want my students to think about their crazy English teacher who sweat over Shakespeare when they were in ninth grade. Learning is a process, an experience, and I want them to feel the learning happen, I don't want them to just exist as bystanders on the path. No matter how hard I try though, there are always silent critics. There are always kids in my class who are too shy to talk, to share, and to participate. There are not as many now as there were when I started, but some remain. I continuously wonder what those kids think of me as a teacher. I wonder if they don't speak because they think I am too crazy to even deal with, or if they are somewhere else in their minds. There are times when I wish I could hand out comment cards like restaurants do. I wish I could tap into the kids who make me wonder how I am really doing. However, I have had the rare opportunity to catch a glimpse into the minds of a few of my silent critics on separate occasions. The mother of one of my students brought one such occasion to existence.

Teacher workday at the close of each school year is a sea of textbooks, papers, deadlines, inventories, dust, and clutter. It can be utter madness. One year I went to my mailbox during a break from checking in textbooks and completing the inventory for my classroom. I was hoping to find it empty. Rounding the corner of the mailroom I saw the shadow of papers in the space underneath my name and I sighed, thinking I could not escape the school year until the very last moment. Inside I found the usual, forms on top of forms, mixed in with more forms. But there was something else. Amidst all the forms I found a card with my name written in script across the front. I knew the handwriting had to be a mother's pen. I had memorized the handwriting of my administrators and counselors, leaving only a parent, and mothers are usually the ones who write. On the walk back to my room I turned the envelope over and over in my hands, wondering what could be inside. I ran through the catalog of my last few lessons trying to remember if I said something that could have offended one of my students. I thought back through my grades, wondering which of my students had earned a grade less than what they expected or desired. I admit, my defenses often go up when faced with parental correspondence. While I have received accolades from many parents, aunts, uncles, grandparents, and guardians, I usually look at their *silence* as a sign that I am doing a good job as far as they are concerned. By the time I returned to my room and sat down at my desk I was fairly sure I had been as politically correct as I could be given my personality, and I was stumped. I opened the envelope to find a thank you card. I was perplexed, knowing I had given no one a gift recently. I hadn't done anything that I could think of requiring or deserving a "thank you". Nonetheless, I was staring down at those simple words scrawled across the outside of a card. What I found inside the card caught me off guard.

Miss Gregor,

I just wanted to let you know how much I appreciate your part in my daughter's school year. As a freshman, transitions can often be difficult, but your class seemed to go smoothly for her.

I've heard your name all year long so I know she enjoyed you class. ("Miss Gregor said…" & "Well, Miss Gregor feels…") I realize that Sarah is a quieter student, but I just wanted you to know that you've had quite an impact on her this year. And I've never learned so much about Romeo and Juliet!

Thanks so much again and good luck in your teaching career!

Sincerely,

Beth Richardson

The mother of one of the shyest, most reserved students I had encountered had written me a thank you card. One of my students, a girl I had barely heard say more than "here" when I called attendance, carried home what I taught her in class and shared it with her mom. She taught her mom about *Romeo and Juliet*. She had taken my passion for Shakespeare and developed a passion for him too; or at least enough of an interest to teach her mother the play we were working on in class. What had I done that had made such an impact on this child who never vocalized anything in my class? I knew then that just because the students don't all say so, they hear you; even the ones who you can never be sure are listening. They hear you; and you are important. This is an incredible lesson that all teachers should have the privilege of learning. There have been days walking down the halls to my classroom when I have felt like I could do no good within the walls of my school. I have often felt like I didn't know enough, wasn't good enough, and that I should have stuck with business. But then there are days like that teacher workday, when affirmation comes unexpectedly and quietly. There are those days when even the quietest of students speaks sternly into your ear, telling you, "Keep going, it is important, it is working." The days when you know that you have made a difference to at least one child make all the days of doubt worth it.

*

Kelsey has an extraordinary imagination. She is in the middle of writing her own book that blows my mind. As a sophomore in high school, Kelsey has achieved with her writing what some can only hope to. She has the ability to translate what goes through her head into fantastic stories of fiction. She brings her stories in for me to read and puts due dates on them because I am such a procrastinator. She wants my comments on her work. The truth is, her work is fabulous. I am amazed by her ability. Kelsey told me once that I am the only person she lets read her work, she does not even show it to her parents. I know what it is to trust someone with your writing, and I am grateful that Kelsey trusts me with hers. She has a gift, and I am fortunate that she shares it with me.

Deserving the A

Monica is a bright spot in any day. She is full of life and charisma and she lights up my classroom when she walks into it. I have known her as a member of our high school student council and I have known her as a student in my class. I have always liked Monica because she is a likable young woman. She smiles at everyone and makes those around her happy. She is loved by her peers and respected by them as well. When we got back from spring break the first thing she did when she came into my room was give me a hug. Monica is the kind of kid that would be a parent's dream and a teacher's savior in a room full of students who aren't awake enough or are too apathetic to care about what is going on around them. She is the kind of student teachers can count on because she always has something to say, she always does her work, and she is not afraid to put herself out there for the good of any teaching or learning experience. In a place where a teacher has to try hard not to have favorites, Monica makes that struggle even more difficult because she is so exemplary.

I knew Monica for a year before I had her in class. When I found out she would be one of my students, I was excited but also a bit apprehensive. When you get to know a student in a setting like Student Council, there is a different set of rules than in the classroom, a different way of handling everyday situations. I looked forward to having her in class, though. Monica's character made me know that she would be just as much of a pleasure to be around in class as she was when decorating a gymnasium for a school dance. Sometimes it is hard to describe a student, because they seem unbelievable to those who don't know them. Monica is genuine. She is a real person. She is not a student who walks around trying to mold herself to the crowd, making up whatever person she thinks others will like the most. Monica is also extremely mature. When I talk to her I feel like I am talking to another adult, because she is so much more than one would expect of a high school student. But she knows how to be a kid, as she is one in her heart. She can have a serious conversation and show a real side of wisdom and poise and then be silly and make you laugh if you are having the kind of day that could use a good laugh. She can sense those kinds of days, and she makes them better. On top of everything, Monica is an athlete and a scholar, a leader in her class and in the school. She truly is one of the best and brightest, despite the cliché. How could I help liking a student like Monica? How could any teacher not like someone who comes to school to get an education instead of a date, someone who is pleasant because it comes naturally? I do like Monica, as a person and as a student. Do I like her better than some students? Yes. Is that wrong? I don't know. I also don't know how someone could remain totally unbiased in this profession. I spend an hour a day with each of my students, which is more time in a week than I see my own mother at times. The students who pass through my door are a part of my life while they are in my class, and they remain in my mind and heart when they walk out my door. It is impossible not to develop feelings, positive or negative, for them. But the real question is this: if I like a student, do they get an A? Absolutely not. Some of my favorite students have failed my class. Some of the students I adore have earned zeros on some of my assignments. I would love for all of my students to pass, for all of my students to be happy with their grades, but sometimes that isn't the way it all works out. Calculators and computerized grading systems don't lie and they don't have feelings, which is why I use them. I care about my students and their education too much to give them grades they don't deserve, because I know it will only hurt them in the future. All of my students are equal in that respect.

After the first quarter that I had Monica in class, her friends told her that she only got an A in my class because I like her. Students make excuses often. When their grade is not as high as they would like it to be they become critical of others' grades. The concept that teachers do not give grades, students earn them, is lost on many students. I have said it more times than I can count. Teaching honors students as part of my schedule has shown me the importance of grades to students and parents alike. I once had the parent of an honors student schedule a meeting with me based on a test grade her son earned. She spent about a half an hour in my room explaining to me that her son simply didn't understand the material, though he had never once asked for help or clarification. Then she just looked at me, waiting for me to fix it. She never said it out loud but I knew that somewhere inside she wanted me to change his grade. I have never understood why students and parents want grades that are not deserved. Some people cannot grasp the concept that some kids are A students and some are B students, in fact there are even C and D students out there. All kinds of students are valuable as individuals. Parents and students can often make teachers feel obligated to give out grades but when conviction and ethic does not allow for this, the teacher becomes the enemy. I have rubrics and scales to justify all of my grades. All of my bases are constantly covered. I compute my grades by computer, so there is little room for error. But, there are always questions and crying and fighting, as grades seem to be the focus of so much in the classroom. I won't venture to say that a world without grades at all would be a better place, that would simply be too idealistic.

One of the biggest problems with students is their need to compare themselves to one another. Kids want to know that they are smarter than someone; they want to know that there is someone out there who is less than they are. That is human nature I suppose, as survival of the fittest is a concept still at work in today's society. The truth is, there will always be someone who is smarter, faster, thinner, prettier, and better. Dealing with that fact is often difficult for teenagers. When teens spend their life in an egocentric place, they cannot handle being surpassed. Sometimes, teenagers want to be the best no matter what, and when they aren't they best, they make excuses. Monica is not one of those people. As if she wasn't perfect enough already.

When Monica's friends taunted her by saying she received her A because I liked her, she came to me very concerned. It seemed that her friends had her believing their ridiculous accusations about her grade. She sat down next to my desk and spoke softly with a perplexed look on her face.

"Did I get an A in your class because you like me or because I really deserved it?"

I was a little taken aback. I have had students question their grades many times, but I have never had a student question an A. I explained my grading process to Monica and let her know that I would never assign an A based on how I feel about a student.

"I just don't want a grade I didn't earn."

She wanted to make sure that she earned the grade she got; and I assured her that she earned her A and was a very strong student. She was ready to give the grade back. I could see in her eyes that if I would have said, "Yes, Monica, you should have had a B but I gave you the benefit of the doubt" she would have made me change her grade. In front of me sat a student who refused to take less or more than she deserved. She wanted her grade to be a reflection of her own work, and she would be proud of whatever grade it was. She was not going to take something that wasn't rightfully hers. I don't know of many students who would show Monica's integrity in this day and age. I don't know many students who would question an A rather than blindly accept a grade that has been called into question by someone else.

Monica is unique because of this and many other circumstances. She has integrity beyond what she realizes and a lot of students, and their parents, could learn something from her. Probably everyone could learn something from Monica. We have all taken credit we do not deserve in our lives. It is human nature to want to be good at something, and to be recognized for something. That desire can get the best of anyone, maybe at some point in her life it has or will even get the best of Monica. But on a rainy Wednesday afternoon in my classroom, Monica refused to take something until she knew she deserved it; and that, is something special.

*

A true conversation with a student:

STUDENT   I can't believe you "writ" me up!

ME   Actually, I *wrote* you up.

STUDENT   Whatever. Everyone thought it was funny.

ME   But it was wrong. *Turning my back to put a book away.*

STUDENT   *(to the class)* I fucking hate her.

ME   Out in the hall.

As I followed the student into the hall I thought to myself, "At least the grammar in the *insult* was correct."

Who You Callin' Freak?

During my first week in the classroom, Alex called me a freak. Right in front of an entire class full of students whom I was trying to trick into thinking I had myself totally together, Alex called me a freak. Alex was the kind of kid who would tell you anything, whether you wanted to hear it or not. Alex was rough around the edges and sometimes in the middle too. He was one of our school's original "bad boys". He smoked, he drank, he only came to school when he felt like it, and when he *was* at school he was not interested in being there. He was a teacher's worst nightmare. I heard stories about him from colleagues before he walked into my class. His was a name that was synonymous with trouble. When I got my class lists the year I had Alex in class, my stomach twisted into knots and I braced myself for the fight of my life. When Alex walked in the door on the first day of class, he was everything I had expected. He swaggered in with his attitude as big as the chip on his shoulder. It was obvious that he was a ladies man, as all the girls in class stopped dead in their tracks at the sight of him. He sat in the back, which would not last after all that I had heard about him. He wore a look on his face that simply said, "I dare you." I tried to hide the fear I was feeling. I was a new teacher, new to the nuances of students like Alex, and I had not yet figured out how I would handle him. I was concerned for the rest of my class, knowing that Alex held in his hands the ability to make teaching as well as learning difficult. He was a smart ass from the start and extremely sly. He knew how to talk when I wasn't looking and while I always knew he was up to something, it was nearly impossible to catch him. He could change course dead in his tracks and put on the face of an angel, all the while thinking up his next scheme. And when, after only a few days, he called me a freak, I was certain everything I had heard about him was absolutely correct. But I didn't have all the information necessary to understand Alex as a person.

Alex was definitely a tough young man to have in class, but now as I look back on it, it was all worth it.

After I got to know Alex I asked him why he called me a freak. He told me it was because I came in all "hard assed" and he didn't buy it for a minute. He knew I wasn't as tough as I tried to make myself seem to my students. It was scary really, the way he had seen right through me that first week, because he was right, I wasn't as "hard assed" as I had tried to seem. There are various types of students in the microcosm of the high school. I have learned the distinctions from my students. There are the preps, the kids who wear nice clothes and drive fancy cars. There are the freaks, those kids who don't wash their hair because they want to see how people will react to the smell. The stoners, who want to see how people will react to a totally different kind of smell. You have the brains, those kids who worry more about their grades than they do anything else. The band nerds are the kids who are talented at music, so the other kids make fun of them for that talent. The jocks like to be tough in any situation, beating their chests and high fiving each other in the halls. The cheerleaders look like they are on their way to a club in the middle of the day. The "goth" kids dress for a funeral every day and draw strange symbols on their notebooks and themselves. The "posers" change their looks more often than they change their underwear. The partiers laugh about how they got away with drinking a twelve-pack last weekend before the football game. Then there are the troublemakers, for lack of a better term. The troublemakers will do all the things no one else will do. The law rarely restrains them and their idea of fun is anything they can get away with; which is usually anything they want. The troublemakers have a reputation to uphold in school. They have to prove themselves as people who don't care about authority, who challenge it for all of the students who aren't brave enough to do it themselves. I have had all types of students in my classes. However, it is the troublemakers who aren't afraid to tell the teacher, "Hey, you aren't as hard assed as you try to seem."

Alex was the original troublemaker, the one that all the others looked up to and tried to emulate. For some reason there some teachers who get along with the troublemakers. For reasons I cannot explain I am one of those teachers. During my own high school experience I stayed away from those kids and fell into the hated "prep" category. One would assume that the kids who are most like the student I was when I was in high school would be the ones I identify with and sympathize with the most. But it is the kids no one else gives a chance who I have ended up having a soft spot for, and Alex was no exception. Alex was the boy who had been branded with a bad rap. It became obvious to me early on that many of his actions were efforts in trying to live up to his reputation, because he didn't know who else to be. Not many teachers gave him a chance because before he walked into a classroom door, the teacher on the other side had inevitably heard a story or two about him, and usually the stories weren't good. I have, for some unknown cause, reserved judgments of these kinds of students. Perhaps this Nick Carrawayan aspect of my personality worked on me just like it did Fitzgerald's famous narrator; for all of the "bad seeds" I have come to know and love have left a permanent mark on me. I look at what some may see as bruised, damaged, or flawed youth as a challenge, an outlet for someone with a big heart and Alex quickly become the recipient of my understanding, and my allegiance.

Students can sense what kind of teacher you are when they meet you. In the same way that Alex knew I was not a hard ass, he knew I was someone he could trust. He knew I wasn't out to get him, out to bring him down as so many other teachers had tried in his past. Because I accepted him for what he was, Alex brought me into his confidence and I learned a lot about him. I learned that his parents were divorced and that both had remarried and started new families. I learned that he didn't feel like he fit in with either family and he was always looking for his true place in life. Maybe it was for this reason that he drank too much and smoked too much pot, or why he always acted in a way that attracted attention, be it positive or negative. Alex needed something from the world he wasn't getting, so he numbed himself with activities that were generally not healthy, and not legal. But I liked him. I found a way to get through to Alex, at least a little bit, by listening to him and letting him know that I was not always judging him, but trying to help him stay out of trouble. I was real with Alex and I let him be real with me. When he told me a story and cussed right in the middle of it the way he would if he was talking to one of his friends, I didn't send him to the office, because I knew that he wasn't trying to be disrespectful, that was just a part of who he was. He respected me because I respected him, and we got to a point when he did swear, that he would throw his hands over his mouth dramatically, raise his eyebrows, and say, "Oops, I'm sorry." He was a good kid, no matter what other teachers thought of him, he just needed to find his place. Alex didn't want to be in trouble all the time and when he did something wrong, he knew it and seemed remorseful. It was as if he didn't know who he was if he wasn't the one who always got in trouble, the one who started and ended fights, who lead instead of followed.

Once Alex got into a fight in my class. The class was watching a movie and a student was not respecting Alex's boundaries. Alex warned him that he wanted only to be left alone, but the other boy continued to push Alex, mentally and emotionally, until Alex snapped physically. Before I could get to the other side of the room the two boys were on their feet and throwing punches. Doing something I had been taught in school never to do, I stepped in between the two boys. All new teachers are told not to put themselves in harm's way because when teenagers explode with anger, they may very well explode on you. But I knew Alex wouldn't hurt me. I stepped in front of the other boy so I was face to face with Alex, my hand extended to his chest. I could feel his breath heaving and see the tears welling in his eyes. I told Alex to wait for me in the hall and sent the other boy down to the office so the two of them would be separate. When I got Alex into the hall he calmed down quickly. His tears showed me that he didn't want to fight and he kept telling me over and over that he told the other kid to just be quiet. Alex was tired of being pushed when he stood up to fight. I saw a kid before me who had been pushed around for most of his life, trying to find a soft spot to land. Apparently, my classroom became his soft spot. From that point on, when he was angry and thought he would snap, he came to me rather than get into a fight. He sought solace in my room and in me. I was glad to be that for him. It was my way of keeping him safe and out of trouble at least for a little while.

A dreaded day for me came when Alex came to my room and told me he was moving to Florida. He was going to live with a man who was once married to his mom. He was thrilled and couldn't wait to leave and make a fresh start. He had found his place, which is what I wanted for him, but I was crushed. I couldn't believe I was going to lose the little thug. I couldn't imagine a day when he didn't walk into my room and say he was late for a class and if I didn't give him a pass he would get suspended. I couldn't imagine not hearing him yell down the halls, or even call me a freak. I had grown used to being his safety net and not realized that he had also become mine. It had happened underneath my nose, naturally, but I didn't see it until I was faced with losing it. Alex was my constant reminder that I taught because deep in my heart I cared about my kids, not just their education, but them as people. Alex made me feel like I was doing something good, something worthwhile. He needed me and I needed to be needed. Selfishly, though I wanted him to find a real home, a place where he could be whoever he wanted to be, where he could start fresh, I didn't want to lose him. Alex spent most of his last day of school in my room. He went to his other classes long enough to turn in his books and then came back to the place where he could be himself. Before he left for the day he handed me his textbook, and reluctantly I took it from him. Flashing through my head were all the times I had written him passes or let him get away with something I knew I shouldn't have. I remembered sitting with him at my desk when he tried to do his work, for me, no matter how much he hated it. I remembered the look on his face when he did well in my class. As he was about to walk out of my room for the last time, he looked me square in the eyes and said, "Thank you for all you have done for me. You are the best teacher I have ever had." When I hugged him I cried. I told him I would miss him and expected him to visit. And while I knew I would most likely not see him again, he said he would be back to see me and for a brief moment I believed him. Alex was someone I cared about very much and I knew I would always worry about him. I wanted him to be okay, and I wanted him to fit somewhere, because he deserved it. I watched him walk out of my room under the flood of my own very unprofessional tears and I was sorry to see him go. That selfish part of me wanted Alex to stay in my class forever, though I knew it would be better for him to go somewhere and start over. I wished he would turn around and say it was all a bad joke, but Alex didn't turn around. And then he was gone.

I was updated from time to time on Alex through some of his friends. He tried to e-mail a number of times, but that potty mouth of his could not get passed the filters on my school e-mail account. I heard at first that he was doing really well. Reports said he was having fun and things were just as he had hoped they would be. I was happy and sad at the same time because I was beginning to understand that Alex would not come back. Then, one day, I heard he *was* coming back. Life had not been going as well as Alex let on. He didn't fit in with his stepfather and his new family in Florida, so he was returning to live with his grandmother. I always wanted him to come back but I was not happy at the news. His last ditch effort to make it work for himself had failed. My heart ached for him. I couldn't imagine what it would be like to roam around the country wondering when you would find someone who wanted you no matter what. I wished for him to have the unconditional love that every child deserves, and though he was almost 18-years-old and tough on the outside, I knew he had to be hurting on the inside just like a little boy would be in his situation.

I continued to hear about Alex from his friends, who all said he would stop in to see me just as soon as he could. He wasn't coming back to finish high school. He was going to get his GED. Then I started to hear the rumors about hard drugs. I was constantly worried for his safety. I wished he would clean up his act and not prove right all of the people who told me he was no good. Then I heard the news that I had feared would come, but was never pessimistic enough to let myself believe would really happen. Alex had been arrested and was in jail. When I found out I was so angry with him. How dare he? I had warned him so many times to get his act together, to use the chances he had been given in life, no matter how few and far between they were. And where did it get him? Jail. What could he have done? How seriously had Alex screwed up this time? He had been charged with burglary. The police had found Alex and a friend in a woman's house at 11 o'clock at night and the house had been trashed. Both Alex and his friend were awaiting arraignment. My heart sunk at the news, because I couldn't believe Alex was stupid enough to burglarize someone's house, and because I couldn't bear the thought of him in jail. The stories around the high school were that it was all a misunderstanding. Alex said he had permission to go to the house because he stayed there for a while and left speakers behind. I wanted to believe it, but it was difficult since he was sitting in a jail cell. Alex's arrest was the kind of news that tortures a teacher who can never heed the advice to leave school issues at school.

One day, as I stood outside my door, making sure the hallways were safe for small freshmen to navigate through, a girl I barely knew walked up to me and handed me an envelope.

"Alex wanted me to give you this, I went to visit him yesterday."

It was a letter from Alex. I was touched and eager to hear how he was and what was really going on. I opened the envelope to find four pages written in the hand of a student I had to practically bribe to write when he was in my class. Alex's letter caught me up first on what had been going on in his life. He told me that he didn't fit in with his stepfather's family and had tried living with his real dad, who was too into drugs to be any kind of father. He said he was lonely in jail and it was hard to be there because he didn't have the support of his family. My heart broke for him; he was alone and in jail and didn't even have the love of his family to hold onto. Swallowing the lump in my throat I read on. In the midst of his ordeal, Alex had done something for me. He read his first book. Alex told me the name and author of a book he had read while in jail. He said it was the first time he had ever read a book all the way through. Alex was 18-years-old when he read his first book. He said he thought I would like to know because I had always tried to get him to read. He was already planning on reading a second one too. This young man, who no one wanted, read his first book because of me. I had done something right. He ended his letter with these words:

I miss you a lot! You're still the best friend/teacher!

Love,

Alex

I saw the good in him as always, even from a jail cell. He was starting to get it. He was starting to reclaim his life because it wasn't too late, it never is.

Despite being so angry with him for getting himself arrested, I was proud of Alex. It had taken an extreme circumstance for him to find out the real truth in life, that we all make our own ways, our own paths, our own destinies. No matter how difficult, and how much life can throw in our faces, we all have the capabilities of reinventing, refreshing, and regrouping ourselves. As I read and reread Alex's letter I knew he could never know that by simply reading a book inside his jail cell, he made every day I had ever spent teaching worth it. He showed me that maybe some of my kids wouldn't get it while they were in my class but eventually they would, and if I had any part of any of my students getting it, that ever illusive "it", each day in the classroom would be worth the work. I still think about Alex calling me a freak and smile a little because maybe he was right, maybe I am a freak. Our differences are what often lead others into thinking any of us are freaks. I am different because I put my heart out there for kids who have been tossed aside, and sometimes it hurts. Often my colleagues think I am foolish for letting my kids get to me the way they do but I don't care how silly it makes me seem. I love my kids, and I love my job. And if that makes me a freak, I am okay with that.

*

During Teacher Appreciation Week, I got this letter from a student.

Dear Mrs. Whitmire,

I would like to take a few minutes to thank you for teaching me this semester. I know I am not the best student, nor do I retain all of the information you give, but I can say, without you and your class I would no longer be a poet. It was your passion for poetry that rekindled the flames that had only months ago burned out. Some people say poetry should not be taught in class because it kills a child's desire to take part in it. Our course on poetry has only intensified my desire to involve myself in such beauty. Whether it appears this way or not, your class makes me think. It deepens my desire to learn the English language and utilize it in ways one would not think possible. I think you are a beautiful woman and a great teacher. It is teachers like you who are remembered for years to come and thanked when former students make it to success.

Thank you,

Dinnelle

Markus

Dealing with students who have learning disabilities is both a challenge and a joy. It is often difficult to find innovative ways to teach students who learn in unconventional ways. There are some students who can't sit still long enough to take notes for twenty minutes, or even five minutes. Some students have good ideas for essays, but simply cannot translate the ideas from their brains to the paper in front of them. Often times, reading silently in class is next to impossible for some kids. It is excruciating to watch students who want to do well struggle and sometimes fail because they have disabilities holding them back. It is a joyous thing to see the look on a student's face when they get something they didn't think they could get. When you work around and through the disability and see the light go on, see the "a-ha" look come over a struggling student's face, it is an experience well worth all of the hard work on your part and on theirs. I wouldn't trade my work with my students who need a little extra help and attention for anything. I can handle the extra paperwork and extra meetings because in the end, teaching someone who didn't think they could learn, who other teachers didn't think could learn is an experience that cannot be matched.

Markus was on an Individualized Education Plan when he came to my class. He had been identified with a learning disability in both writing and reading. So, like many students who struggle with any subject, Markus was not incredibly fond of English. Markus had plans to attend a vocational school during his Junior and Senior year in high school and I had him as a sophomore. In other words, Markus simply needed to pass my class in order to get enough credits to go on and learn a skill that would help him be successful in life. There is a stigma attached to vocational training in ours and in many schools. All "normal" high school students assume that the students who leave their home school for vocational opportunities are dumb. It is a difficult stigma to break due to the fact that many of the students who pursue vocational training at our school are those with learning disabilities, thus those with comparably lower grades than their peers. I am in no way saying that students with learning disabilities are dumb, this is simply the cruel and untrue label that teenage minds have created. Few of the students who label those who choose a vocational path realize that after graduating from our school's training program, many of the students will make more money than I do to teach those students who are college bound. Markus fell victim to being labeled because of his status as a student with "special needs", but unlike others, he spoke out against the label.

While Markus was in my class I gave all of my students the task of writing and delivering a speech. After reading Martin Luther King, Jr.'s *I Have a Dream* speech, each of my pupils was to think of a topic they felt strongly about and then deliver a speech on that topic. I was worried that all I would get were speeches in favor of the legalization of marijuana or the abolishment of all homework in classrooms across America. I was pleasantly surprised to discover that my students cared about a wide range of issues. Some wrote speeches about medical testing on animals or the harmful effects of smoking, and Markus wrote his speech on kids with learning disabilities. I didn't know how strongly his label, or the way others reacted to his label, had affected Markus, until he revealed his speech topic.

When the day came for Markus to read his speech, he was too uncomfortable to read it in front of the class. It was a deeply personal subject and he felt too vulnerable to stand in front of peers who had made him feel like less than he was and vocalize the hurt that resulted from such an experience. I allowed a friend to read for Markus, knowing from the look in his eyes that he needed a break on this one. As his friend read the intensely personal speech, I watched Markus. I wanted to connect him with his words for one, and I also watched him because I wanted to see the true effect of what he wrote on his face. He looked down most of the time while his speech was being read and there was hurt in his eyes. He had not written the speech to simply fill a requirement, he had written it because he had something to say about the way his peers looked at him and other students with learning disabilities. The entire class was silent as Markus's speech was read; they listened to their own faults and must have wondered if they had ever said or done anything to make others feel ashamed for having a learning disability. I kept my eyes on Markus, so proud that he had spoken up about something that had obviously hurt him and so sad inside that he had ever felt like less than the amazing person I knew him to be.

After class I saw many of Markus's classmates approach him to congratulate him on such a moving speech. Some hugged him, some patted him on the back, and some just gave a soft smile that said, "I am sorry" or "I understand". It was truly incredible that Markus had, with his words, moved his classmates into action, valuing a kid who was different from them without judging him, something that in high school can be a challenge too great to measure. I gave Markus a hug after the class thinned out and told him I was proud of him. He smiled. I could see the triumph in his eyes.

Markus went on to vocational training as he planned and will graduate with the training he needs to make more money than the teacher who was more proud of him than she could really express. Money isn't it though, Markus has confidence that he can do anything he wants to do and he can be successful at it, despite his learning disability. Markus still comes to see me when he can, and he is still kind, gentle, and good in all the ways that make someone a true humanitarian. He is the kind of boy I would want my daughter to marry if I had a daughter. Markus touches my heart because of how genuine he is. He knows how to be a gentleman. He is a hard worker, he is polite, he is respectful, and despite what some people may have made him believe, Markus is smart. I hope he knows that.

*

I have never had Marie in class. We met in study hall and she has the sunniest personality I have ever encountered. She smiles enough to fill a room with light. She is genuinely a sweet person. There are times when students can make your day without spelling all the words correctly in a composition or memorizing a famous Shakespearean soliloquy. I don't know what kind of English student Marie is. But I know what kind of person she is; the kind that has made many of my days. Every so often Marie stops by my room on the way to class. When she sees me she tells me she has missed me and gives me a huge hug. Sometimes, she gives me hugs when I need them most. She is kind and sweet, and she makes me smile. Who knew students could make your day?

Behind His Humor

In teaching, there are students who see it as their responsibility to keep you on your toes. For me, Chandler was one of those students. Chandler made his way into my class as a lanky sophomore, full of life, and ideas, and shenanigans. Chandler's peers saw him as the original funny guy. I cannot count the number of times he changed the mood of a room because of his uncanny ability to make people laugh. Once, during Chandler's sophomore year, I was sitting at my desk while the students were reading from their textbooks. I was working on grades and had not noticed Chandler get up from his seat at the far side of the room and creep to a computer. Suddenly, the silence of the room was pierced by the sound of the printer spitting out a freshly inked sheet of paper. The printer's location next to my desk allowed me to simply look up and reach for the paper from my chair. As I eased toward the printer I assumed that another teacher printed something to my room in lieu of a printer that worked somewhere else. But when I picked up the sheet of paper, I saw something I didn't expect. I read the text on the sheet now sitting in the middle of my desk. Out of printer had come the following statement: "My feet smell? How could they? Since when have feet become their own organism with individual parts such as a nose or a brain? My feet stink." Confused, I looked up at a class of silent readers and wondered what in the world had happened. And then, from across the room, I caught the eye of a lone student sitting at a bay of computers. He looked up at me and gave me the slightest sly smile, waved, and then walked to his seat to continue reading. The sly smile was Chandler's.

Printing out humorous quotes became a tradition that belonged solely to Chandler. I knew when Chandler was in a particularly curious mood, because my printer would spit out strange messages at random. We soon found a spot in my room to display Chandler's musings, and he began to hang them up.

Students, teachers, and administrators alike walked into my room and were quickly confused and amused by Chandler's display. I am sure plenty of them thought I was ridiculous to display what seemed to be nothing more than nonsense. Maybe it was ridiculous to them, but to me, it made perfect sense to display the creativity of a student who was wonderfully weird. By the end of Chandler's sophomore year he kept a binder in my classroom filled with the craziest of his sayings. To this day I don't know why he wrote them, how he came up with them, or what most of them meant, but they were a part of who Chandler was. I was in no position to quell Chandler's expression and I didn't want to. When my students create and explore and express, I find it my responsibility to celebrate that, in unique ways, ways that fit each of my students. A section of my classroom where Chandler could display his creations and his thoughts, was my way of celebrating him. Teens grow and express themselves in different, sometimes odd ways, but it is all a part of who they are. I liked the quirky parts of Chandler; they made him interesting. They made me see a student who was thinking outside the box, and having fun while doing it. Why suppress that because some people might think it is strange?

Aside from his humor, I have come to know a different side of Chandler, one that not everyone gets the opportunity to see. Chandler is a passionate young man. He is, as an 18-year-old, more politically savvy than many people considerably his senior. He looks at issues that matter to him and he takes a side based on educated opinions. Chandler cares about what is going on in the world around him. He does not possess the apathy that so many students his age do. He works to make himself aware of the world so he knows how to change it. Chandler is more unique in this regard than he ever could be because of his odd expressions. Chandler would rather engage in a political sparring then drink an illegal beer with his buddies. Chandler doesn't do what is cool, he makes his own path and he follows it, no matter how lonely it may get. Chandler makes it cool to be different in a place where different often leads to destruction. Where people blend in, Chandler sticks out because of his values, his beliefs, and his unwavering ability to be his own person in a sea of sameness.

Chandler writes poetry too. One day he came to me and handed me a thick stack of papers. They were his poems, tons of them, and he was there thrusting them at me to read. I urge my students to write for their own reasons and while most reject the thought, some exercise their creativity in various ways. I try to convince my students to find an outlet. I allow them to know that growth and learning can come from creativity. I have fought with educators who say that creative writing does not have a place in the English classroom. I have tried to show my students that they can free themselves from so much if they write through their problems, their thoughts, their joys, and their sorrows. Chandler took my suggestions for writing to a new level. Chandler found his outlet in poetry, and I was fortunate enough to have a rare glimpse into that outlet. He was so proud of himself when he handed me his work. I could see in his eyes that he was handing me something he had put all of himself into. He was handing me a piece of himself that he did not share with everyone. Chandler trusted me with something that was terribly personal to him. It is often difficult for students to share their work, even their academic work. But to share personal thoughts can sometimes be paralyzing for students. Chandler, however, opened up the window to his private self and allowed me to look inside.

The poems Chandler gave me were powerful. Some of them were rough around the edges, but they accomplished the goal set forth for them, vocalizing Chandler's feelings on any issue at any given time. His poems spoke of love and rejection, and inner turmoil. They spoke of the struggle that so many people Chandler's age must go through, never knowing how to vocalize it. Chandler gave voice to the issues that I know to be so common in teens. When I read his poetry I had an image in my head of Chandler, alone in a dimly lit room, pounding out his thoughts on the keyboard of his computer; tirelessly immortalizing his thoughts on disk and then paper. It was as if he was speaking for a generation who didn't know how to speak for itself. But his peers didn't even know that he was speaking for them, perhaps they weren't even sure what they had to say. Chandler fit under what his peers thought of him, and few knew what really lie beneath his surface. He was the boy who fell on purpose in a crowded hallway to make people laugh, or the kid who danced in front of the class when he got a good grade. But he was also the poet, who knew the name of his own demons and faced them head on. Chandler was the poet who knew his turmoil and the turmoil of his peers and was not afraid to put it into words. I was moved by Chandler's poetry. I was impressed that he was not afraid of his own emotion like some young men his age can be. Most of all, I was intrigued by Chandler's duality, and the way he seemed to have a multifaceted aura about him that some could not see.

Chandler didn't try to be extraordinary, he just was. He was when I first met him, and remains, a true original. He loves life and he lives that life. He allows himself to be afraid and angry, in love and heartbroken. He puts himself out there in a world that has the potential to reject him, but rather embraces him because he is so magnetic in his ways. Chandler is special in ways that go beyond the norm, breaking the rules and making up new ones as he goes.

Chandler is the person who taught me that not everything has to be defined to be wonderful. Chandler defies definition. He taught me that teenagers have the capability to be so much more than they let on, so much more than what people think the "typical teenager" is. He also taught me that it is okay to let people laugh at you, only if you laugh first and loudest.

*

Nathan went to Italy for two weeks and missed about eight days of class. When he left I told him to bring me something back. I was joking, but he did. He brought me a Murano glass ring, which his sister helped him pick out. He said he felt weird bringing a teacher a ring, but it was small and cheap. I said thank you, but reminded him that I was already married. Nathan is a fun-loving kid who knows how to take a joke. You find those kids quickly as a teacher, the ones who can take some fun natured ribbing and the ones who can't. Nathan and I have a unique relationship, he takes my sarcasm and runs with it. Once, trying to be sarcastic himself, Nathan told me he wanted a new English teacher. The next day I sent him across the hall to one of my colleagues and told him that I had changed his schedule. He thought I was joking, and I was, but I left him there the entire period. When he walked out of the other class his own class was standing in the hall with me to greet him. He laughed it off and told me he would get me back. I don't doubt that he will try. Students like Nathan let you have fun with your job. They break up the monotony of every day in a high school. Students like Nathan make my job more fun than I thought it would be.

Unexpected Guests

In the middle of this process, the process of writing this piece, something happened to me that I knew I had to include here. It is funny how things come at you in life that you do not expect, things that change you and affect you. This chapter is devoted to a student I never expected to write about. His chapter was brought about by his mother, with whom I had a poignant conversation. It was today actually. Not today for you, who knows what happened during the today somewhere in the future when you are reading these words. But today, as I write this, something extraordinary happened.

My phone rang during my planning period. Many teachers have a similar reaction when the classroom phone rings. "What's wrong now?" The walk from my desk to the phone is always a slow one as I try to guess who might be on the other end of the line, and what they might want from me. I feel all too often that less and less of my time is spent focusing on the students I am in school to teach, while I am forced into the sometimes-demanding bureaucracy of education. So, on the walk to the phone I allowed a hundred different scenarios to play out in my head: my lesson plans were not state standard savvy enough when I turned them in; my study hall was getting a new student; I was reassigned to bus duty; I had to cover another teacher's class during my planning period; I was being evaluated by an administrator...

"Hello."

"Hi Mrs. Whitmire, this is Mrs. Kanings (one of the school counselors). Mrs. Stevenson is here and we were wondering if we could stop up to talk to you."

Stop up to talk to me? During my planning period? Unannounced? What is this? Has education turned into an ATM? Parents drive up, push a button and whatever service they demand pops out in an instant, is that what we have been boiled down to as teachers? Drive up service? Are we not professionals who deserve the same courtesy as a banker, or a lawyer? Would someone walk into a law office and say, "I'm sorry I didn't call first, but I need a lawyer now for my hearing in 10 minutes, and I have decided you will be the one. Let's go to court"? I don't think so. This is not the way the world worked the last time I checked. I have to make an appointment for everything. I don't just walk into my hairdresser and say, "I need a haircut" and sit down in the chair. Damn. I am a professional. Since when do I have to be at someone's beck and call? I don't get paid enough for that. That's right, I don't get paid enough for that; do the math.

"Of course you can stop up. Give me two minutes. Good bye."

Rarely can teachers say what they really think in education. For example, when a parent asks, "What can my Johnny do to get an A?" I can barely resist the temptation to say, "Johnny has to be smarter to get an A. Thank you, good-bye." Better yet, "Why is Susie failing?" I have to chew on my cheek in order not to utter, "Because Susie is lazy and doesn't do any of her work." The truth is, I do care about students but have little tolerance for parents who want me to give their children grades they do not deserve or are not capable of earning. So, more often than not, I bite my tongue, or chew on my check, or pinch my own skin when I fold my arms. I thought, after the request from the counselor, which method of torture I could employ to keep politically correct for an unannounced parent whose son accomplished little more in my class than drawing breath, which is why he failed. I actually had less than two minutes to think about it. It seemed that seconds after I hung up the phone in my classroom, there was a knock on the door.

The counselor feigned apology, though I knew she had to have been the one who suggested the party of two come up to "stop in". I would meet the mother of my failed student with the best smile I could muster. I didn't even have time to rise from my desk before the duo charged in and took seats in student desks next to mine. I didn't have time to even utter a word before the mother spit out the reason for her visit. Mrs. Stevenson wanted to discuss the last assignment of the quarter her son failed. He failed the assignment because it was not completed as it was intended to be. I gave my freshmen a persuasive speech assignment. They were instructed to decide on a topic they would like to persuade someone about, and then give a speech in front of their peers on that topic. The written part of the speech was not what the students were graded on; it was the oral standard I was looking to impart upon them. I gave students opportunities over three days in class, to volunteer to deliver their speeches. I had quite a few students who were not at all reluctant to speak, and some who waited until the last day when they knew I would have to drag them in front of the class and force them to speak. Mrs. Stevenson's son did not volunteer, so he knew he would have to speak on the last day. However, just before class, Mark Stevenson came into my room and gave me the written copy of his speech saying that he was too ill to be in class and needed to go to the nurse. I wrote him a pass, and he left. Mark failed the speech.

Mrs. Stevenson began speaking emphatically about the current condition of her son. As she began, I feared that she had come into my classroom to tell a trumped up sob story in order to save her seemingly lazy son. My fears were assuaged only moments after she began speaking. I was not sitting in front of a woman who would make excuses for anyone. She was tough, but not in a coarse way. I could tell that she didn't take anything that had to do with her son lightly, especially the F he got in my class. Mrs. Stevenson wanted to know if Mark would have passed my class had he done his speech. I quickly calculated his average with a passing grade on his speech. Had he given his speech, Mark would have passed the quarter. And then Mrs. Stevenson told me the whole story.

"I am trying to save my son's life."

The sound of her words made me shudder. The emotion was building high in her. I saw faint wells of water in her eyes as she spoke, but she was stern, not frail, and persistent in her words. She pointed at me as she spoke, and for one brief instant I thought her gesture symbolized her anger at me. But she was not angry with me. Her rage was pointed at that which she thought threatened to take her son from her. She was not explicit about what she felt was stealing her son from her arms. She looked at me with narrowed eyes and said, "I think you know what I am referring to." I was fairly certain that she meant drugs. There are a lot of problems teens have, and while I know that drugs are not necessarily the largest, when a parent is worrying about a child in a life or death situation, usually they are worried about drug use. Mark's mom said that she was starting to make the necessary changes and one of those changes was the group of friends Mark ran with. She said she knew she needed to take care of that problem. She was serious.

What I saw in Mark's mom's eyes was electrifying. It was inspiring the way she spoke of the fight she was willing to wage on the danger her son was involved in. I saw in her a mother who loved her son unconditionally, through his problems and shortcomings. I saw a mother who was fighting for her son, even though he didn't seem to want to fight for himself. Mrs. Stevenson was focused on the goal of winning back her son and I knew she wasn't going to lose. There was a part of me though, that wondered what I had to do with Mrs. Stevenson's fight. I wasn't sure why she had come to see me. She could have called me and asked why Mark failed the class, but something brought her to my classroom to speak to me in person. What part of the equation did I fall into?

"I want you to know something about the speech you assigned Mark".

The reason began to crystallize in front of me. Mrs. Stevenson began to tell me how Mark had researched his topic and put a lot of outside class work into it. She said he was interested in what he decided on for a topic. There was the meaning for Mrs. Stevenson's visit. She was trying to change her son's grade. I had begun to think so much of her since she first walked into my room. I didn't want to believe that she came to see me to try to bully me into passing her son after the fact. This couldn't be it. Could it? Had I tragically misjudged Mrs. Stevenson?

"After you gave Mark that assignment, his father and I saw our son again for the first time in a long time. We saw the boy he used to be and it was amazing. No one has been able to reach him in the last year. But *you* reached our son. You created a spark in Mark that we hadn't seen in so long and for one shining moment, we had our son back. I wanted you to know that you succeed in reaching our son. I wanted you to know that you had him for a moment and it was wonderful. You were the only one to reach him. Thank you."

The words seemed to appear like a bubble over her head. I couldn't believe them as they resonated in my ears. I was the only person who had been able to reach their son? I was the only person who was able to turn the light on in a boy who was falling fast while his parents fought to catch him. I tried to speak. I didn't know what to say. I thought I should say thank you, but I could not wrap my voice around the words. I could feel the lump in my throat growing as Mrs. Stevenson repeated the words again, as if to make sure they really soaked in. I reached a child that no one else could. By giving Mark an assignment, one that I thought would meet standards, help the students in a variety of ways, and maybe, just maybe be fun for them, I brought him out of his darkness in a way that stunned his own parents. He came out of the shadows for my class, to work on a project for me.

So why hadn't Mark delivered his speech? The list of medical issues facing Mark was startling. As his mother rattled off the pain, the sickness, he had been experiencing, never being completely sure what was wrong with him, I couldn't imagine a 14-year-old living with such enormous medical problems. He was sick the day of his speech, but he never told me what was going on. Mark kept what was happening to him hidden from me, and only told his parents what happened when he got his report card. His mother had record of the fact that he was sick the day of his speech. He was afraid to say something. He took the F.

Mark's mom did not want me to change his grade; that was not why she had come to my room. She told me that if Mark "screwed up" he had to accept the consequences. She revisited a time when I threw Mark out of my classroom. He came to ask me about a grade but did so in a very disrespectful manner. I told him he needed to think about the way he treated people and showed him the door. Mrs. Stevenson told me that she supported me in the decision to make her son leave my room when he was rude to me. Later he told his mom what he had done and said he felt really badly about it. She was not the kind of mom who was going to make excuses for her son and she respected me for trying to teach him a lesson. She came to my room only to tell me that her son did the work necessary to complete the writing of his speech, and that he truly was sick on the day he would have given it. But above all she was in my room to thank me for reaching her son.

I have dealt with my share of parents but have never met one like Mrs. Stevenson. I had never seen a mother in such a battle to do what her son needed, whether he knew he needed her or not. She was going to win her son back from what lured him away from his family and a normal, healthy, teenage life. She was tough and loving, outspoken and passionate. Mrs. Stevenson gave me a rare glimpse at what teaching can do for some kids. I would have never known on my own that I reached Mark Stevenson. He is a quiet boy, who sometimes does just enough to get by. He slips under a lot of radars and doesn't create a fuss. He is easy to miss. And maybe I would have missed knowing Mark's real story without the help of his mom. I know I would have.

I hate the fact that I was annoyed when Mrs. Stevenson arrived in my room. But I would be lying to say I wasn't. It was a real reaction to a situation I didn't fully understand. I didn't know what she was coming in for, and while I thought it was to make my life harder, she was actually coming to tell me how I had made her life and the life of her son a bit better. I am thankful to Mrs. Stevenson for coming to my room and telling me what she did. I am thankful for an assignment I gave without thinking it could help a young man in a fight that he probably doesn't even understand. I have not felt quite so satisfied in many other teaching situations. But all I did was my job. I went to school to teach kids, and that is what I was doing with my persuasive speech assignment. But I have come to know that I am a teacher for more than just teaching. I am a teacher to affect kids, in any way I can. I am a teacher so I can show kids they are okay when others tell them they are not. I am a teacher so I can let kids know someone cares when they think no one does. I am a teacher to help kids, even when I may not know I am helping them. The job description is to teach, but the person in me knows that I walk into my classroom each day for many other reasons.

*

The kids in his class make fun of Tim sometimes. They poke at him because he spends so much money on clothes and has a very odd way about him. He talks too loud and stands too close. I have seen him look around to see if the other kids are watching when he makes a scene. But he makes school fun. Sometimes he walks into class doing an Irish jig. Tim is a sweet kid. He makes me CD's to listen to and stands out in the hall with me before class. He means well. Tim has not yet learned that he is good enough as a person not to have to dazzle others with expensive clothes and a high tech cell phone. He has a lot to offer simply by being who he is. I hope he comes to know that soon.

A Sheep in Wolf's Clothing

Jonathon is a dichotomy. He has long hair and listens to loud music. He is the kind of kid you look at and assume he will give you trouble. Once, Jonathon pulled the fire alarm in the high school and got suspended. When teachers talk about kids in the lounge you would expect them to talk about a kid like Jonathon as a troublemaker, but aside from the fire alarm mishap, he is no such thing. Jonathon taught me an important lesson. He showed me that there is no way to look at a teen, or their actions, and know what kind of student or person they are. He taught me not to judge my students though I never thought I had been guilty of it before I met him.

I have always considered myself an open-minded person. I have preached the gospel of acceptance all of my adult life. But I was guilty though, of judging my students. When I first started teaching I looked at the teens walking through my classroom door and I thought I could tell what kind of student they would be. I saw many of the same labels that existed when I was in high school, the same labels my students use for each other. When I saw a person walk in with dark makeup around their eyes, chains on their jeans, topped off with a studded necklace, I assumed that person would not care about school. When I saw a well-dressed person walk through the door I imagined that person as an individual who would care about their grades. This is not something I like to admit but something that I have grown beyond. Jonathon helped me grow beyond my judgmental ways. He allowed me to become the open-minded person I thought I was. The open-minded person I am now. I thought I was more than I was. Jonathon brought me to reality and showed me a side of myself I didn't want to see, a side of me that I refused to admit existed. When Jonathon walked into my classroom he was loud and boisterous with long hair and dark clothes and I thought, "Oh dear, what does he have in store for me?"

127

I judged Jonathon before I knew him. When he first came into my room he talked all the time and I had to stop class repeatedly to quiet him down. He laughed loudly, disrupted those around him, and often times he made inappropriate comments. He didn't care about school, I thought. It was obvious to me. He came to class to dazzle others with his humor and to have a good time at the expense of anyone around him. However, academically and personally, he exceeded any expectation I could have had for any of my students. Jonathon is one of the most inquisitive and intelligent people I have ever met. I have had him in class for two years and in that time I have seen him grow into an exquisite young man. He loves Shakespeare, now there is a student after my own heart. When we were about to read *Much Ado About Nothing* I told Jonathon's class that I was going to show the film version first to give them a visual image while they were reading later. Most students would find news of a movie before text music to the ear, for some of my students are foolish enough to think they need only to watch the movie and not read the play. Jonathon, however, is not like most students. He did not want to watch the movie before he read the play because he didn't want it to taint his reading of the play. He wanted to be able to make mental images and fill in all the blanks with his own imagination. I was floored. I just looked at him in dumbfounded amazement. Before me stood a sophomore in high school who did not want the easy way out, but the way that would make him think and allow him to expand his mind. Jonathon was excited about the opportunity to read something he had never read before, to go somewhere in learning that he had never been.

During his time in my class, I was stunned by Jonathon on more than one level. I was stunned that I had so tragically misjudged him and I was stunned that he was such an exemplary student – not because of my first impression of him, but because I have never seen a student as sharp as he is. Jonathon is not an Honors student, he does not get all A's, and sometimes he can be more than a little disruptive. But I have seen him carry a class discussion. I have seen him analyze literature so profoundly that I think he should be the one teaching the class. I have seen him hunger for new experiences, new knowledge. He is truly a teacher's dream, in a package that has in the past been confused with a teacher's worst nightmare. I wonder what Jonathon would say if I told him my first impression of him. He would probably laugh and tell me what he thought of me at first. Jonathon is going to do amazing things in life. He can be anything he wants, no matter what people think he should be. I labeled him unfairly and learned a valuable lesson from him. Brains, determination, kindness, wit, charisma, and focus come in all shapes, sizes and colors. I have learned since meeting Jonathon that sometimes, no matter how much you polish it, a rotten apple will be mushy on the inside, but bruises do not always ruin the fruit. Jonathon came to me in an atypical package and turned out to be an atypical student, and a splendid surprise.

*

Why do students need a teacher who is willing to dig into a story with them to get to the heart of it? Think of what we would miss if we all looked at only the surface meaning of literature...

When asked about Act I of *The Miracle Worker*, the play about Helen Keller, Brooke responded with the following:

"Mel, it's a deaf girl, that's it, that's the story."

Drawing Him Out

Nick was the boy no one seemed to want. He came to me as a foster child living in a group home and was placed in my class during the middle of the year. It is a struggle to make a student melt into a class after it has already been in session for half a year. It is especially difficult, however, when that student comes from a situation like Nick's. It is hard to imagine being a teenager and being pulled out of your parents' home. I can't fathom being thrust into the home of strangers, rarely even being able to visit your natural family. I do not know all of the circumstances that resulted in Nick's placement in foster care. What I do know is that Nick carried a card each day on which I had to evaluate his performance for the day. I had to comment on how well he paid attention, if he completed his work for the day, and if he had any missing assignments. I later found out that the results of the card Nick had to have signed by all of his teachers determined whether or not he could visit with his biological family on the weekend. When I learned the latter piece of information I could not imagine a situation that would warrant such treatment. I wondered how any child could be expected to perform in school under such pressure. How could anyone succeed under the threat of detachment from his or her own family? Shouldn't family be accessible at all times? Family is not a reward, but something every child deserves.

When I first met Nick he did not say much. He requested that his seat be in the back of the room. I knew instantly that this was not so he could talk to others, because he did not seem to socialize with anyone in class. It was clear to me that Nick wanted to keep to himself. He did not want to be bothered nor did he want to bother anyone else. He wanted to be left alone. I watched him over the first few days that he spent in my class. I saw in him a boy who didn't want anyone to see him, or perhaps a boy who had grown accustomed to

133

not being seen by anyone and didn't want to break with tradition. Nick rarely made eye contact with students or with me. Also, Nick rarely did any work. Sometimes he kept his head down, and sometimes he stared out the window deep in thought. At times he was working on something but I felt certain it was not class work. I never pressed him though, because I wasn't yet sure how he would take it. Before handling this type of situation, I felt it necessary to assess it. I didn't want to yell at Nick, I wanted to understand him and approach him in a way that would be appropriate for him and for his unique situation. So I told myself that I would give it a couple more days of observation and then I would sit him down and discuss his lack of interest or activity in class.

As I waited, assessing Nick's situation, I received tragic word from his counselor. Nick's biological mother had been struck by a car and killed. My heart broke in an instant for this boy, this student I barely knew. His life had already been filled with such hardship, such turmoil, and now his real mother had been taken from him. I didn't know what to do for him. I didn't know what to say after he returned from the absences due to his mother's death and funeral. I was in what I believed to be an impossible situation. I felt the only recourse was for me to handle him gently and try to fight the seemingly impossible battle to understand him.

In the days following his mother's passing, I discovered that Nick had a passion for drawing. All the times when it was obvious he was working on something in class, he had been drawing. When I saw some of Nick's drawings I knew that he had a real talent. He was meticulous. He cared for each line on the page, each stroke with his pencil was full of purpose and thought. Nick revealed his talent to me in a subtle way. He sat close to my desk when we watched films in class and didn't hide his drawings from me. He sat back so I could see them without much strain. He did not want a fuss and did not seek out compliments the way the average teen would. There was no one at home to put his drawings on the refrigerator. There was little normalcy in Nick's life at all. I knew then the defining characteristic of Nick. Nick was not a student who wanted to learn in school. He was not even one of the students who doesn't particularly want to learn but will do it anyway because they are supposed to. Nick was the type of student who did not do his work, was not afraid of the consequences, and had absolutely no interest in school. So, as a teacher what do you do with a student that refuses to learn? Can you really make a student learn something they are not ready or willing to ingest? I have grappled with these questions day after day, even before I met Nick. If a student is in your class and there seems to be no way to reach them academically, what do you as a teacher do? How do you force it? Do you force it at all? I don't think there is any right answer to these questions. Once again, I never read this chapter in any of my college textbooks. I found out through experience that so much of what we learn as novice teachers is idealistic. Idealism didn't work with Nick; there was no way it could. So, with no rulebook, no guide, I had to make a tough decision. I had to decide what I would do with Nick and hope I made the right choice.

I had a few different courses of action I could choose from. I could kick Nick out of class. What would that do for him? Would it teach him anything to kick him out of class? Would he do his work in the hall? No. I could give him an office referral, which would most likely end in disciplinary action from the administration. How would Nick benefit from being reprimanded by the "authorities"? It wouldn't scare him; I had a feeling he had been through worse in his life. It wouldn't make him do his work, and it wouldn't make him an active participant or learner in my class. I could stand over him and force him to work, but how? Should I take his hand in mine and move his pencil across a blank page to make him take notes? How would that help Nick and what would he learn? The truth is, there was little I could do that would *make* him learn in my class.

Through teaching I have learned that students have to be willing to learn. They don't realize it all the time, but they do. They have to be willing to open their minds and let information in or they won't get anything out of school. Even when students would rather be anywhere but in my classroom, if they are learning while they are in class, they are exercising a will to do so, no matter how small that will is. There are various reasons why students are willing to be a part of their own education. Some feel they don't have a choice, because after all what will they do with their lives if they do not graduate high school and ultimately, college? Some know that their parents expect them to learn in school so they fulfill those expectations. Some want something more for themselves in the future – something more than their parents have, something extraordinary that only education can give them. Some come to school because they know there is a chance they could be arrested for truancy if they refuse. For all of these reasons, as well as some I may never have entertained, I have nearly a full class each day when I go to school. And while Nick, for his own reasons, showed up frequently in my class, he was willing to do nothing more than that.

I decided not to fight Nick. I didn't think I would win and I didn't want to be one more thing in his life that was hard on him. It seemed to me that life was hard enough on Nick. However, just because I chose not to battle Nick, does not mean that I gave up on him. I pushed Nick as far as I thought I could. I reminded him gently when he was missing work and he was receptive at times. He wrote down his missing assignments and every so often I saw a sign in his eyes that said he might do them. The sign usually faded away though, to my dismay, but not my surprise. But I refused to give up on Nick. I hoped against hope that while he was in my class he would absorb some of what I was saying. If he was not willing to learn I realized there was little I could do, but while he was in my class he was at least present. He had to get something out of class. I had to find a way to give him something while he was one of my students.

I knew that Nick loved to draw. I didn't take his pictures away when he worked on them in class. I wanted Nick to have something that was his alone, something no one could take away from him. Nick's art was that something. I wouldn't try to change that. There are different types of students in every class. Sometimes, as a teacher, you find out that some students don't want to learn. This is a reality that is not easy to face as an educator. It is hard to understand students who don't love knowledge the way I do as a teacher. But I had to quickly learn that not all students would share my passion. I had to decide what I would do when faced with a student like Nick. In truth, I may not handle all reluctant learners the way I handled Nick. I would not let everyone draw in my class. Is that wrong? Am I unfair? I don't know that there is a logical answer to those questions. I know that Nick needed something more from me than grammar and a strong foundation of world literature. Nick needed stability. Nick needed someone to tell him that he was a talented artist and that his drawings were worth something. Nick needed to know that he was worth something. If Nick missed all that I had to say on semicolons or on persuasive essays, but he listened to the parts of my class when I tell my students that each individual in this world is valuable to someone; that each of my students is valuable to me, then I would have given him something. If Nick refused to take my knowledge of English, maybe he could take away life lessons from my class. I have wondered many times if Nick has learned any life lessons that he didn't have to discover the hard way. I wanted to give him that opportunity, if nothing else. I wanted Nick to remember that at some point in his life there was someone who took him the way he was, not trying to change him. I wanted him to be celebrated for something, not punished for everything. I think he needed that. If I couldn't give him grammar or literature I would try to give him a sense that he was good at something and that somewhere in the world there would be people who recognized that. I also thought that if I respected Nick, and let him be who he was, maybe he would pick up on some of the English I was trying to teach in class, maybe he would remember some of it down the road, out of mutual respect that I tried to achieve with him. That would be better than nothing.

Some lessons have to be learned the hard way, and the one Nick helped teach me was difficult. It was agonizing for me to discover that sometimes, there are students who fight against learning so hard that you can't fight them back. If you fought your hardest against all of the kids who don't want to learn then you wouldn't have any energy left to teach the ones who do. So how do you make the choice? How do you decide which students get the focus? You don't decide that, the students do. In a way, students are largely in control of their own learning. You can't force a student to study and to retain. You can only give them your knowledge, your guidance, and your help, and ask them to take it – if they don't take it, your hands are bound by their unwillingness. So, are students who are unwilling to learn, students like Nick, wasting their time by being in class? I don't think so. Because of students like Nick I have tried to teach all of my students more than is required. I have tried to teach my students about people and the world around them. I have tried to teach my students about acceptance of themselves and of others. I have tried to teach them the lessons they might not learn at home. Some may say that it is not my job to teach my students anything but elements of grammar and literature. I say that if I have the opportunity to make my students more human while they are in my class, I will do that. I make no excuses or apologies. I do what I think is right for my students and for me. There is too much that happens to students when they walk outside my room, therefore inside I will give them an environment of safety, respect, acceptance, and peace. I am clear that my job is to be their English teacher, but as a person I feel I owe them more than that.

So Nick sits in my room and he draws. At times he does his work. He is more open with me than he used to be. Nick and I have a good relationship. I accept him, I respect his boundaries and I encourage him to do what he loves. In turn, Nick has never disrupted my class, he has never blatantly disrespected me as a person, and he shows up on time every day. I take what I can get with Nick, which in often a lot more than I get from my other students. I can say that I have learned a lot from Nick. I know that I may not reach all of my students academically. But I also know that I can reach my students in other ways, and still provide them with valuable lessons and information. I know that it doesn't make me a bad teacher when one of my students refuses to learn. There are so many factors in students' lives that affect them more than we as their teachers know. I decided not to fight Nick, but to be on his side, because I don't think he has had too many people on his side.

As I was finishing Nick's chapter I got a phone call from Tara Wyland. She told me that Nick ran away from his foster home and had, at that time, been missing for five days. I thought he was sick. I thought he would be *coming back. Now I have no idea where he is and I don't know if I will ever see him again. He left his home on his bike and according to some of the other kids in the foster home, he met a man in a car and took off. Apparently he stole a Game Boy to sell for $100. I was stunned to find out about Nick running away while I was working on his chapter. I thought I would have a better way to end it. I didn't think I would have to confront the thought of him being out on the streets somewhere, possibly in danger. I wonder if I will see him again. I wonder what will happen to him. Right now I wish I had a few more moments with Nick the last time I saw him. I wish I could have reminded him of some of the things that are in this chapter – that he is worth something even if it doesn't always feel that way. This is the sadness of my job; caring so much that you become vulnerable to situations beyond your control. Is it worth it though? Yes. Each heartache is worth it to know that somewhere out there are the people you have tried to reach, on a number of levels. I know that Nick is out there somewhere and I know I did my best where he was concerned. Now I can only hope what I did for him made a difference; though I may never know for sure if it did or not.*

I got a drawing from Nick the other day. Apparently he had been working on it for days before he ran away. It was supposed to be a gift for me that he could give me himself. He left it with his Special Ed teacher and when she gave it to me I burst into tears. He signed it, "From your partner, Nick." I think of that drawing as proof that I did get through to him in some way. I use it to tell myself I must have made a difference and that makes all the difference in the world to me.

*

Ray is very special to me. She was in my class during my second year of teaching. She was an average student who never tried as much as she should have. She didn't always work to her potential. But something about her tugs at my heart. She is rough on the edges. She is moody and sometimes has a huge chip on her shoulder. Ray is also the kind of girl that other girls victimize because she is cute and all the boys like her. It is agonizing to sit with her when she tries to figure out why some people are so cruel to her and why so many girls talk about her behind her back. Ray spends a lot of time in my room. When she is done with her work in other classes she comes to see me, to talk or to grade papers for me, just to be there. When she walks into my room I smile because I genuinely like her, I want to be around her. Sometimes when she has had a bad day I put my arm around her and stroke her hair, trying to make her feel better. I see the person I might be as a mother when I am with Ray. I want to take care of her, make her feel better when she is sick or sad. I want to yell at the girls who make her feel bad about herself. My relationship with Ray is the kind of relationship I would want to have with my own daughter. Imagine that, a woman who never wanted kids can see what it would be like to be a mother, all because of a student. All because of Ray.

The Banana Incident

Kim was in my class during my first year of teaching. She had a terrible habit of eating in class all the time. She knew she wasn't supposed to eat in class and had lunch right after she came to my room but she told me she was always too hungry to wait for lunch. Since I had a rule that food was not allowed in class, students who did eat in class at least tried to be discreet before they were caught. But not Kim. Well, maybe she tried to be discreet, but while most students secretly dined on something small like candy, Kim ate sandwiches, chips, and once a banana.

One day, after days of kindly reminding Kim to wait for lunch to eat, I caught her eating her banana. I looked at her and she stopped chewing instantly. As if by stopping the movement of her teeth, she could fool me into thinking that she wasn't really eating in class. However, her cheeks puffed out, full of banana, and I could see the peel in her lap. Our exchange went something like this…

"Kim, don't chew in front of me."

Muffled laughter from Kim, with a mouthful of banana. No chewing yet.

"Kim, don't do it. Don't chew your banana."

More laughter behind bulging lips. Still no chewing.

"I bet that banana is getting mushy in your mouth Kim. I bet it feels gross."

Kim now begins to laugh harder, holding her mouth closed, but not yet chewing.

141

After a few minutes of banter...

"Kim, are you ever going to eat in my class again? Don't swallow, just answer."

Through more laughter, Kim manages to shake her head to signal no.

"Okay Kim, swallow that delightfully, mushy, soggy banana."

By the time the banana slid down her throat the whole class exploded with laughter.

"That was so gross!" Kim declared as she laughed even harder.

Kim never ate her lunch in my class again. However, she did move on to applying her makeup in class. Once, she dropped a whole container of blush on my floor. She looked at my with eyes that said, "I'm sorry." Less for spilling and more for getting caught putting on blush in class. The whole class erupted with laughter. It became obvious to me that Kim was willing to do just about anything but what I wanted her to do. She was not trying to be disrespectful, she seemed to just be trying to optimize her time. She was a sweet girl, the kind you can't help but like even though she was always doing something she shouldn't do. I was always on the edge between wanting to hug Kim and strangle her. She tested my patience. She wrote her papers in sparkly pink pen that I could barely read because of the color. Instead of doing her work, she wanted to talk to me about life and what she did over the weekend. She had no secrets and no shame, an interesting combination. She moved away and left a Polaroid picture of herself with me. I still have that picture in my desk and look at it every once in a while. I miss Kim.

*

A good example to use when students ask, "Why do I need English class?"

In my sophomore class, we were reading a play and in order to get the students to understand how to paraphrase Old English language, I told them to imagine themselves in the situations of the characters and write how they thought their peers would speak the words in today's society. I used the names of two of my students as an example and said, "Try to imagine how Shane and Troy would have the same conversation as say, Caesar and Brutus." As a joke, and to see if Shane was paying attention, I added, "Well, maybe don't use Shane." Hearing his name, Shane looked up and said, "What? I talk good."

Teaching With OCD

I have OCD, Obsessive Compulsive Disorder. This is not a happy disease to have when you are a high school teacher. Everything in my classroom has a place. When something is moved, I know it. My college roommate used to move things in our dorm room just slightly when I was home for the weekend. She would take pictures, shampoo bottles, anything she could find, and move them even a millimeter to see if I would notice when I came back to school. I always noticed, but I wasn't officially diagnosed with OCD until recently. It is difficult to be around a person with OCD without noticing that they have it. Needless to say, my students are very aware that when something is out of place in my classroom, I notice immediately and it has to be fixed. I am honest with my students about the fact that I have OCD, I think that is important. I don't want anyone to think that I am ashamed to have this disorder. It doesn't make me weird, it doesn't make me a freak; it makes me different from most people. I have come to know that different can be fun. I want my students to know that when there is something about you that sets you apart from everyone else, it is not a bad thing – it is nothing to be ashamed of.

Is it strange that my students know about my OCD? I have never really thought anything about it. Is it too much information for them? Is it too personal? I don't think so. It affects me and I think they need to be aware of the things that affect me when I am in charge of them. I think that is important. I am a person; I have quirks; that is who I am. I know when my students are on medication for conditions that may affect them in my classroom. OCD affects me in the classroom. It is my own rule that we are all people in my classroom, including me.

There are some drawbacks to letting my students know I have OCD. Two of my students always tease me about the fact that I cannot handle anything out of its place. They have told me since my first year of teaching that they would somehow get into my classroom and rearrange it someday. No way. I lock my door when I leave to go the restroom – another part of the OCD. I do not leave anything unattended. Yet these girls have continued the joke. They have said it would be their ultimate prank, for me to come to my room one day and find it totally unrecognizable.

Once, when I was monitoring a study hall, one of the two girls came down to say that one of her books was locked in my room. I reluctantly gave her the key to go retrieve her book, explaining the procedure of relocking the door more than once, and didn't notice that she didn't come back for at least 20 minutes. I also didn't notice that her accomplice, her best friend, who happened to be in my study hall, signed out to use the restroom at the exact moment that I gave my key away. Now, I am quite observant in my own classroom, but in a study hall with 120 students it is difficult to know every move. So, I had no idea that on the second floor of the high school, my room was being rearranged.

When I walked into my classroom after study hall I couldn't speak. The entire room was changed. All of the desks had been moved to face the opposite side of the room. My own desk had been taken from its home and moved all the way across the room. My paper bins were moved. My files were dispersed to new locations. Everything was changed. It was my worst nightmare. On the chalkboard was a message from the culprits. I wish I would have written down what it said. It was a poem describing to me the fact that they got me the way they always promised they would, but they still loved me. I had to laugh at the fact that they pulled it off right under my nose. I gave them the key to my room. I let my guard down and they did what they promised they would. Many of my other students stopped by to see what had happened and all of them were astonished that I was taking it so well, that I wasn't furious. I did, however, spend the next half hour turning the room around, knowing I couldn't leave for the day with my classroom in disarray. While I switched everything back to the way it was, I wondered myself why I wasn't mad at them. I came to the conclusion that they made the day interesting for me. They made life interesting for me. That is what my students do; they make life exciting.

*

Chandler wrote this poem for me before he graduated:

You sparked me

The time has come and I cannot speak
Here it is again and I cannot think
My thoughts rush freely in our final week
Put a lump in my throat, I cannot drink

It is hard to push away the laughter
You helped lift me out of eternal doubt
I broke down in tears and you came after
Your smile and independence helped me out

Every minute I see you, I laugh
You make me look past the once lonely nights
You split my once painful life in a half
Now I stretch to reach new heights

This is my way of letting you believe
I do not want to ever see you leave

**It's *almost* a sonnet (despite a few syllabic discrepancies). He wrote me a sonnet!

Teaching Through Tragedy

I was a first year teacher on September 11, 2001. Perhaps the most frightening day in American history unfolded just as I was getting into the groove of my new occupation. I have reflected on the day many times and realize each time the uniqueness of my position on that day. I remember my mother telling me where she was when John Kennedy was shot, and my grandmother recalling her activities on the day Pearl Harbor was bombed. I have had many people ask me where I was when the World Trade Center Towers were attacked. I was in my classroom. It was 10:00 a.m., fourth period, by the time I heard anything about what was going on. My fourth period students walked in and asked me if the Pentagon was on fire because of a bomb. They had heard a rumor. I laughed. It was an insane notion.

"Yeah, right, the Pentagon was bombed, like that would ever happen."

That was my reaction. There was no possibility of truth in the rumor that had filtered to my students as I saw it. I couldn't conceive of it. I actually laughed out loud. It was my own arrogance as an American citizen. I lived in the country that no one could touch. I lived in the country that others feared, not inflicted fear upon. I laughed.

Moments into the period there was a knock on my door. Another teacher in my department was stopping by to let me know that we were all allowed to turn on our televisions and watch the news if we wanted to. What was she talking about? I had no idea why our administration would offer to let the school watch TV for the rest of the day. After the explanation from my colleague I realized what my students told me must have had some measure of truth in it. The world stopped for a split second as I stood in my doorway with my back to my class wondering how in the hell I would explain what was going

149

on to my students. I didn't have time to think. I quickly edged toward the TV as I told the students that there had been an attack on the Pentagon, as they heard, as well as the World Trade Center Towers in New York. The oxygen was sucked out of the room immediately. We were frozen as I turned on the TV, only to see the image of New York City, with smoke painting the skyline and the Towers there, ablaze.

We did not turn on the TV in time to see the planes crash into the Towers, and I am thankful for that, though we watched the image replayed over and over again. There was eerie silence as I watched the news in horror. My mind raced. I did not know what was happening. I did not understand. And neither did my students. Oh god, my students. I looked out at their faces, staring at the images of terror before them. I did not know what to say. I just remember the deafening silence in the room, pierced by the voices of reporters on the scene and around the country. What was I going to tell my students? How could I explain something that I could not understand? Inside I was panic-stricken, but I knew that I had to hold tightly to my composure. I would have to address them. I would have to find answers to give them. Years from that moment in my classroom, people would ask my students where they were on September 11th and they would remember that they were with me. That was an awesome responsibility.

I sat with my students and tried hard to understand what was happening to our country. I tried to find the words to tell them that uncertainty was the only certain thing in my head. I explained to my kids that obviously America had been attacked and that I knew nothing more than they did at that moment. I told them that the best thing to do was to watch the news and talk to their families when they got home. They were afraid and there wasn't anything I could do about it, because I was afraid too. I tried to be strong. I told my students that everything would be okay, that our nation would be defended. I didn't believe what I was saying. I didn't know how to believe anything as I watched America's sons and daughters rush into fire and smoke in order to save lives. We were being attacked; not just the people of New York and Washington D.C. or the people on the planes used as giant bullets at an unsuspecting target; every person in the country was under attack – our freedoms and our safety. Our greatest fears were coming true before a nation of wide eyes. September 11, 2001 was the only day that I have lied to my students. I told them something that I didn't know to be true. I told them they would be safe.

All day long students filtered in and out of my classroom. I never turned the TV off. I couldn't imagine teaching grammar in a time of national crisis and I told my students so. There was nothing I could teach them that was more important than what was happening. We watched the second tower fall. We watched people run through the streets of New York, screaming and covering their faces, shielding out the ash and smoke. We watched the tears and the smoke and the ash stain the faces of our fellow man. I sat with my students and tried to take it all in as they did. I tried the impossible. I tried to comprehend it all, to answer the question why.

To be in a classroom full of students during one of the defining moments in American History was an experience I cannot adequately describe. It was sunny outside. The sun filtered in through the windows of the room, creating a glare on the TV. We watched. Motionless. Breathless. Speechless. Students began to ask more and more questions that I could not answer. I watched them watching the aftermath of a full-blown attack on their country. I wondered if they understood the significance of it all, and quietly hoped they did not. As fourteen and fifteen-year-olds I was sure theirs would now be a generation full of war. I knew they would see the atrocities of war over and over, eventually not being able to remember what their lives were like before images of hate and fighting and death. I witnessed a different part of history that day. The faces of children against the backdrop of tragedy was my history, my memory, my "where were you when" reflection. The innocence of a child brings life into perspective in so many of our significant moments. The innocence of a child set up in contrast to acts of war is a powerful image. Where was I on September 11th? I was with my students. I was holed up in my classroom with my eyes glued to the television trying to make sense of a senseless situation for kids who looked to me for answers. I was on the phone in my classroom trying to reach a friend living in Georgetown, just minutes from Washington, D.C. I was on the phone with my husband hoping that he, as a television news producer, would have some answers. I experienced the terror with my students, I shed tears with them, I worried with them.

September 11th and the days following make up my most trying moments as a teacher. I remember explaining to my kids that there were obviously people in the world who hated us, for the freedoms we have and the lives we live, but that the hatred could not take away what was fundamentally ours: our sense of self, our hope, our faith, and our dreams. I told them there were certain things that planes cannot crash into. I tried to restore in them what people they didn't even know were trying to take away. I don't know if it worked, but I didn't know what else to do. I had to restore my own faith in my safety, and I knew my students needed the same thing. We helped each other through a time of crisis unlike anything we will ever witness again. There are moments I look back on in teaching that make me smile, moments that make me laugh, and moments that make me cry. Looking back on September 11th there is little expression now. There is a moment of stale remembrance plagued with turmoil. There is a moment of question: "How did I get through it?" "How did I look the students in the eyes and try not to scare them with my own terror?"

I was in my classroom on one of the most tragic days in American history. I was in a place that is safety and home to me. I tried to make a safe place for my students that day; in a world that felt so dangerous, so bruised, so broken. That is my legacy from September 11th, that was my part in helping America heal, being there for my students.

*

If my students read this book and did not see the inclusion of the following lesson they would say I left out one of my most defining characteristics as a teacher. I am adding this for them.

As a teacher, I try to make my students aware of what they say and how they sometimes victimize people without realizing it. One word I will not let my students use in class is the word "gay". High School students in general use this word in description of anything they dislike. However, in my classroom they cannot call each other "gay" as an insult, they cannot say that my assignments are "gay", or homework in general is "gay". Although they try to trick me sometimes and say, "Gay means happy", I am too smart for them. I tell them that in society the word "gay" has come to be used as a label for those individuals who are homosexual. Therefore, since "gay" is used to describe a group of people, they cannot use it as an insult because they are in turn insulting homosexuals by implying they are bad. So I tell them that until society starts to use the word in the correct way, they cannot use the word in my room. They ask, "What am I supposed to do, change society?" My gleeful response, "YES! You finally understand!"

Curtain Call

It's funny the way life handles you sometimes. You end up in a field you never thought you would enter and then when it comes time to leave it, you can't imagine doing anything else. When I found out that my husband was offered a job in Chicago, I didn't want to go. I had found my place, as a teacher, one who changes lives, and I wanted to stay. The feminist in me screamed at me telling me, "You don't have to follow your husband everywhere he goes, you are a strong and independent woman, cut your own path." And a more quiet voice from somewhere inside told me to look through his opportunity to find an opportunity of my own, which is what I did. Part of what I have tried to instill in my kids is a willingness to go after and catch their dreams, even if they are scary, even if it is hard. I thought I should take my own advice. I thought I should give Chicago a try, give the writer in me a chance.

Leaving the place you have come to know as home is hard, especially when home feels a lot like who you are. I am a teacher. I can't cut it out of me, I can't change it. This is who I am. I have been cleaning out my room for the last few days, filling boxes with the remnants of the last three years in my classroom. It is a different view from the other side of the desk, one that has taken me on a wild ride. Saying good-bye to my students has been the hardest part for me. I have waded through tears finding the right words to tell them how much they mean to me, though I am sure my own shortcomings in this language can never adequately capture their place in my heart. My students, all of them, have been amazing people. They have been people with stories worth telling, lives worth living, and dreams worth chasing. I am a profoundly different person now than I was when I stood in front of my first class. My heart is a little bigger, my skin is a little tougher, and the wrinkles and laugh lines are becoming more defined. During my first year of teaching, I actually found my first gray hair.

My students have all taught me something, about life and about myself. They have all enriched me in a way I can never repay them for.

When I slowly had to tell my students that I was leaving, it was more than difficult. Ashton ran out of the room crying. Mike stared at me, waiting for me to tell him that I was lying. Rachel refused to talk about it, saying she couldn't imagine coming to school without me there. Meredith wondered who would "save her life" in her senior year if I wasn't around for that. Mel kept reminding me that there was no one like me, saying she was lucky to have me while I had been there. I know some of my students must have been happy that I wouldn't be in school. As much as some of my kids have loved me, I am sure some of them would rather have been taught by Satan himself. But as the time came for me to pack up and go, I brought all of my kids together in my classroom for one last message. When I say "my kids" I mean those who have found their way into a special place in my heart, those whose stories lay within these pages and some whose stories are waiting to be told. I gathered them together to tell them all the things you tell people you love, making sure they get it before you aren't there to remind them. I cried the whole time and so did some of them. My kids became the reason I got up each morning to teach. My kids made the journey what it was for me. This journey called education is a bumpy one, but one that is well worth the trip.

I have seen a lot since the first day I walked into the classroom. I have seen tears and laughter and learning at its most difficult, and at its best. It has been the experience of my life. I have often wondered how my life would have been different if I would not have chosen this path. There were days when I thought I would never be able to handle another minute, and days when I thought I could teach until I died. It has been a roller coaster of every emotion a person could ever feel. I have not loved every minute; that would be a lie. There have been days when I thought I could never walk back into the building, or my classroom, never face my students again. But in the end, I am a teacher. I am a lot of other things too – but teacher is something that is in me, like my own heart, or my brain. I don't know if I have done things the way I am supposed to, I don't know what "supposed to" is when you are trying to mold and shape lives. For the most part, I have followed my instincts, and I think my kids have turned out okay once I have sent them away from my class and on to their next adventure. There have been days when I didn't know what I was doing – when I had to feel my way through the dark, but I am not ashamed of getting lost once in a while. Because in the end, I have loved my kids. That love has translated itself into passion when I am in the classroom. I hope I have given them some of my passion – for literature and writing, and for learning. If not, maybe I have been able to give them a passion for life or at least the knowledge that they can find their own passion. And when I lock the door to my classroom one last time, I will know I have done the best I could do. That's all I can do. That is what I have asked from my kids; that they give me their best, and I have given them mine.

AFTERWORD

In life, it is rare to find someone who greatly impacts you. I am one of the lucky ones who did not only meet one of those special people, but I got to know her, learn from her, and be inspired by her. In my high school experience I met a miraculous woman who was there to guide, mentor, teach and be a friend to me when I needed one.

I was fortunate enough to find someone who believed that a child could be led down a good path, a constructive path, a loving path. I have seen many students, with problems most adults cannot even fathom, seek her for advice, a kind ear, or just for a friend. It takes so much for a person to let go of stereotypes and see past what most never will. Because of this, Mrs. Gregor-Whitmire is what most of us hope we can become.

The story of her experiences and challenges with students is not just a recollection of events that occurred. It is the story of so many students who have been impacted and changed by her. No, this isn't even a story; this is a life, an empowering life. This is a life that I, and many others, hope to one day resemble.

Understand, this is not just a story of a teacher whose students provided her with quirky anecdotes. This is the life of a teacher who has inspired and bettered students. This is a teacher who has gone above and beyond her expected role. She is the true definition of a teacher, mentor, and role model, of a wonderful and real person. This is not a book about how we changed her, but how she helped to make each of us better.

~Ashton Finical

"Anna"

To those who know what it is like to be in the trenches,
fighting for the education America's youth needs, fighting
against what threatens our youth, fighting for what is right;
those who aren't afraid of being in the trenches because it is where
we are needed most. The students hear you and they need you.
I would fight alongside you any time; especially, Anne.

About The Author

This is Kylie Gregor-Whitmire's debut publication. She is an English teacher who chose to bring her passion for words to high school students.

Email the author at demfem1@yahoo.com

Check out the blog at http://kjgw.blogspot.com

Printed in the United States
53689LVS00003B/164